Voodoo Anyone?

How to Understand Economics Without Really Trying

by

Christopher T. Warden

Forewords by M. Stanton Evans
& Malcolm A. Kline

Accuracy in Academia

Accuracy in Academia
4455 Connecticut Ave, NW Ste. 330
Washington, DC 20008
http://www.academia.org

For information about special discounts for bulk purchases, please contact Accuracy in Academia at 1-800-787-4567 or info@aim.org

Design by Elizabeth Jenkins

Printed in the United States of America

10 9 8 7 6 5 4 3 2

First Edition

Publisher's Cataloging-In-Publication Data
(Prepared by The Donohue Group, Inc.)

Warden, Christopher T.
   Voodoo anyone? : how to understand economics without really trying / by Christopher T. Warden ; forewords by M. Stanton Evans & Malcolm A. Kline. -- 1st ed.

   p. ; cm.

   Includes index.
   ISBN: 978-0-9676658-9-4

1. Economics--Popular works. 2. Medical care--Economic aspects--Popular works. 3. Agriculture--Economic aspects--Popular works. 4. Power resources--Economic aspects--Popular works. 5. Crime--Economic aspects--Popular works. 6. Economics—Political aspects--Popular works. I. Evan, M. Stanton (Medford Stanton), 1934- II. Kline, Malcolm A. III. Title.

HB71 .W37 2009
330   2009908611

Dedicated to my parents, family and all my students.

TABLE OF CONTENTS

Straight Down the Middle
By Malcolm A. Kline
January 12, 2009

Accuracy in Academia lost a great friend with the passing of Troy University journalism professor Chris Warden, the author of AIA's forthcoming textbook *Voodoo Anyone? How to Understand Economics Without Really Trying*.

He passed away on January 4, 2009 due to complications from hip surgery. The loss to his expansive coterie of close friends on both coasts and throughout the South is even more incalculable, your servant among them.

I last spoke to Chris the day before Thanksgiving when, as usual, he was in good spirits—upbeat and funny as ever—with plans and enthusiasm for last-minute changes and addenda to the book. AIA featured Chris in an appearance at the National Press Club last July.

Many of the attendees, like his charges at Troy and staffers and interns under his supervision in other jobs, stayed long after hours to hear his insights. Chris always took his jobs and responsibilities very seriously but did not take himself too seriously.

So many of the clichés most of us try vainly to live by Chris actually did. For instance, he worked hard and played hard, mostly golf and the horses.

He practiced informal efficiency. He was one of those rare people who could actually be both informal and efficient at the same time, for example, banging out flawless copy while clad in a Hawaiian shirt with a turtleneck underneath.

We can't find any record of Chris ever having to make a correction on one of his stories. Against the sheer volume of pieces he produced, from newsletters in the 1980s to newspaper columns published last Fall, that level of accuracy is indicative of his professionalism.

Nobody could be more self-deprecating than Chris. When we discussed *Voodoo Anyone?* last year, he said, "Hey, did you ever imagine 20 years ago when we were drinking coffee all day and beer all night that some day we would be doing something useful?"

The truth is, every day of his life was useful, and he did it all—research, reporting, writing, editing, and teaching—often while in tremendous pain. Hemophiliac from birth, arthritic since childhood, Chris frequently functioned while in a fragile or frail condition.

Many years ago, I asked him how he did it. He credited his parents, a pair of remarkable retirees, with teaching him sympathy without self-pity.

He demonstrated the former toward all whom he came in contact with but never showed any evidence of the latter. During World War II, the British placed posters all over London which read simply, "Keep Calm and Carry On."

This is another little aphorism Chris lived by. "Well, the bathtub's full of water, got plenty of batteries and beer, Pop Tarts are laid in, so I think I'm ready for Ivan when it hits, supposedly Wednesday about midnight," he wrote in an e-mail when a hurricane was aimed for the state that he lived in—Alabama—five years ago. "Should be fine," he predicted, "as long as I don't pretend I'm a Weather Channel reporter and venture out into the 80+ mph winds they are predicting." He survived Hurricane Ivan, and, as indicated above, so much else.

An obituary prepared by his family and friends notes that "he is survived by his parents, B. E. (Jack) and Louise, of Nisswa, Minnesota, and a sister, Kathleen, of Minneapolis, an aunt and uncle, many cousins, several godchildren, and all his students."

With the publication of *Voodoo Anyone?*, at least some of the lessons he taught in the classroom will live on as well. "By understanding just one aspect of economic analysis in simple terms, the media can better inform the public," he wrote in the introduction to

Voodoo Anyone? "In turn, people can make better choices in their lives."

The textbook that he left us goes a long way towards achieving that goal. Fortunately, in his too brief life, Chris got to realize the goals he cared about most.

In the quarter century in which I have known him, he always wanted to teach, and did, much more effectively than the professors whom we usually get to write about. Moreover, his students learned.

You can't really die if you leave behind good memories and a life that lessons can be learned by. In my humble opinion, Chris did both, with a vengeance.

Rest easy, pal. I hope that you are surrounded by beer, pop tarts, post times, tee times and every other thing that your heart desires.

Eternal rest grant to him O Lord and Let Perpetual Light shine upon him. May he rest in peace.

Amen.

FOREWORD

This is a book that's long been needed—and is needed nowadays more than ever.

"Economics for journalists" may sound like a dry, academic subject, but as recent events have shown is anything but. With financial institutions, housing markets, the auto industry and numerous others crashing down around us, economic topics in the past few years have come to dominate the headlines.

And these, be it noted, are just the more sensational stories that have lately rocked the nation. Add such perennial favorites as gasoline prices, health care costs, jobless rates, educational funding, taxes, inflation and official budgets, and the prevalence of economic subjects in the news is readily apparent.

Unfortunately, these are subjects that very few members of the press corps are equipped to cover. Most of us are products of liberal arts or j-school curricula where economic courses aren't a requirement. With the exception of reporters for certain specialized publications and a handful of financial/business columnists, we typically haven't been trained in economic matters, haven't thought very much about them, and—if truth be told—haven't cared to.

And, naturally, if the media don't understand such subjects, then the general public that relies on the media for information won't understand them, either. Which of course is precisely the situation that we have today, as economic calamities everywhere surround us, and the whole affair is viewed as a huge, mysterious puzzle to which nobody knows the answer.

This little book can't possibly solve all these problems, nor could even a very large one do so. It can, however, make a solid start toward finding a solution. By instructing youthful journalists in some elementary principles of economics, and their relation to important stories in the news, *Voodoo Anyone?* can begin the process of making the nation's communications media somewhat more literate in their treatment of economic issues.

The author of this study, the late Christopher T. Warden, was eminently qualified to carry out the project. Himself a first-rate economic journalist, he was also a first-rate journalism teacher. As the reader of these pages will discover, he had a knack for putting complicated things in everyday language, using anecdotes and familiar examples that made his points in forceful, clear, and frequently humorous fashion.

I had the privilege of knowing and collaborating with Chris over a span of more than 20 years, first at the National Journalism Center in Washington, D.C., then at Troy University in Troy, Alabama. I thus had a chance to work with him, observe him in action as a professor and see his devotion to his students (and theirs to him). He was born to be a teacher, and was a very good one.

In between these teaching assignments, Chris served for eight years as a top-line staffer at Investor's Business Daily, rising to become the editor of its editorial page. It was at IBD that he honed his own lucid understanding of economic subjects and considerable skill in explaining them to the public. Things that otherwise seemed incomprehensible to many became clear thanks to his common-sense, skillful handling.

This book is a product of Chris' unusual background as a practicing economic journalist and as a journalism teacher. It may be read with profit by young reporters—and maybe some who aren't so young—who want to understand the major stories of our era.

M. Stanton Evans
June 2, 2009

INTRODUCTION

When most people hear the word "economics," their eyes glaze over. Wake up. Hey, wake up. (See?)

But rather than some mysterious, and boring, topic, economics is pretty simple. And once you understand its simple concepts, it's pretty interesting, as well. Almost every topic in today's society has an economic component. Health care, energy, education, crime, and marriage all have at least a touch of economics. And they are certainly issues that can have a profound effect on our everyday lives.

Sadly, though, most reporters these days who cover these topics treat the economic component as too boring to learn and too hard to understand. So you get questions like: "How can we solve the health care crisis?" Usually the answers tend to stress a solution that stems from the very cause of the problem.

Here's a New York Times take on it from July 2007: "But many Democrats also see a strong role for government, including, in some plans, new requirements that individuals obtain insurance and that employers provide it, along with substantial new spending to subsidize coverage for people who cannot afford it.

Or try this one: "Who's responsible for these high gasoline prices?" The range of answers is astounding in its ignorance of economics. Consider this passage from a July 2007 San Diego Union Tribune article on gas prices. "The momentum for falling gasoline prices is slowing," said Judy Dugan of the Foundation for Taxpayer and Consumer Rights in Santa Monica.

Dugan says recent declines had a political component, explaining that she believes the large oil companies sought to dampen growing public rage and the possibility of a consumer-friendly federal energy bill with lower prices.

"Oil companies, having killed almost everything they disliked in the Senate's energy bill, can drop their charade of good corporate citizenship," Dugan said. "It's the greedy oil companies."

"Global warming" or "Because we're running out of oil" also get thrown in. All of which make for good quotes but for lousy understanding of the world around us.

Here's another one: "Why can't Johnny read?" Bad parents, bad teachers, bad security, teachers unions all get offered as reasons for Johnny's illiteracy. To be sure, they play a part. But why are they bad, or better put, of such poor quality? The answer is an economic one, but rarely do reporters delve into the underlying economic causes, again, because it's just "too boring."

But what's boring is the way economics is usually taught —demand curves, formulas and, above all, jargon characterize the typical economics curriculum. Remember the scene in the movie, "Ferris Bueller's Day Off"? The teacher, played by Ben Stein, is asking what then-presidential candidate George H.W. Bush said about rival Ronald Reagan's economic policies.

"Voo...anyone, anyone?" intoned Stein. "Can anyone tell me voo...voo, anyone, anyone, voo...doo economics."

His manner is so dull, the camera cuts to a student drooling on his desk while asleep. Stein, whose father, Herbert Stein, was Nixon's chairman of the Council of Economic Advisers, studied economics and law. So one presumes he understands why the student is sleeping and drooling.

Unfortunately, Stein's parody is funny because it is so true. It is rare the economics professor who strives to bring economics down to its real level—namely, describing the actions of people, often using money as a way to keep score.

This book is designed to avoid that boredom and dull treatment of economics, as well as to provide journalists with the tools needed to understand the economic world around them. By understanding just one aspect of economic analysis in simple, common-sense terms, the media can better inform the public. In turn, people can make better choices in their daily lives.

CHAPTER 1

PRICES

When reporting on some topics, journalists hone in on what it means to a consumer or buyer. Some typical questions:

* "How have you rearranged your budget to deal with the high cost of energy?"
* "Why can't you afford health care?"
* "Will an increase in the minimum wage help you?"
* "Can you afford your monthly food bill?"

This is j-school 101—How does an event or trend affect people? But the typical journalist doesn't follow those typical questions with explanations that make any sense economically.

Economists, in contrast, may explain these matters in economic terms, but they make little sense to the average member of the public. For example, an economist might answer the second question above this way:

"The marginal costs of allocating resources to the maintenance of my health are too high."

Why is that, you might ask?

"As I am basically healthy, the cost of providing the extra units of health care that insurance provides is more costly than the cost of using an occasional unit of health care."

Huh?

Similar economic lingo can be found to explain the other questions, as well. But economists and journalists who repeated them would soon find that no one was listening.

1

So explaining these matters in terms that all can understand is a challenge that all journalists face. To do that, journalists must therefore be able to understand the economics of a situation and translate it for their audience. No, it doesn't require an Economics-to-English dictionary. All it takes is an understanding of the most basic issue underlying the study of economics. Price. Journalists are halfway there when they ask questions about how costs and prices affect consumers. But they come up short when analyzing the answers.

Basic Issue

This chapter will discuss what prices are and the differences between the price of things and the cost of things. Prices, as anyone who has gone shopping can tell you, are what you pay for a good or a service. Simple, right? Stated another way, it's what stores will charge you for that good or service. But prices aren't just some arbitrary number. They are also a signal to buyers. And buyers read those signals and make decisions based on them. Again, simple. Why should I pay $3 for a six-pack of soda at one store, when I can pay $2 a six-pack for the same soda at another store? Buyers read those signals hundreds of times a day and act accordingly. And most of those times, buyers will make the choice for a lower price, right?

If you can save $1 on soda, that leaves $1 you can spend on something you also want, such as a pack of Hostess Ho-Ho's or beef jerky. And if you save enough of those dollars, you can go out for dinner, an adult beverage or a night at the movies. Those lower prices, therefore, encourage consumers to buy a certain product at a certain store. These low prices help explain the success of retailers such as Wal-Mart and The Home Depot.

Conversely, the inability of stores to charge similar low prices has led to their demise. Remember Woolworth's? When prices go up, this sends a signal as well. (We'll get to why they go up later.) If that $2 six-pack of soda goes to $4 or even $10, buyers will probably stop buying it as much. They may stop altogether or look for something else, such as fruit juices or just plain water (in bottles at lower prices or basically free out of the tap).

So when a price is too high in the mind of the buyer, he or she will not buy the product. And if the price goes down, he or she will be more likely to buy it. Couldn't be simpler. And people understand that. They rely on prices to send them signals, and they act accordingly. They don't need to know, for example, that a freeze in Chile has led to higher coffee prices, or that Target has streamlined its inventory process to allow prices to fall. They just look at the price.

What is Cost?

Is price therefore the same as cost? It costs consumers to buy stuff, so they're the same, right? Not exactly. From a buyer's standpoint, any price that he or she pays will indeed be a cost. But from the seller's standpoint, cost is not the price at which goods are sold. Instead, costs are what the buyer has to pay in order to sell the product.

Take that six-pack of soda. The store that charges $2 didn't make the soda, and it didn't appear magically out of thin air. The store had to buy it from a distributor. The distributor had to buy it from a bottler and the bottler had to buy the water, sugar and flavorings to make the soda. You add up all those purchases, plus the costs of renting and heating space, paying people and taxes, and you get the price.

Some of you might be saying, "Yeah, but nobody sells anything for what it costs. How could they make any money?" The answer is, they can't. If they sell a product at a price that is the same as what it cost them to buy the product, rent the space, pay employees and pay taxes, they don't make any money.

Have you ever seen a sign on a store window that says, "Come buy from us. We break even?" Because stores don't exist just to break even, then, they add something to what it cost them for the soda and sell it at that—$2. This addition, or mark-up, represents the profit the store is trying to make.

'Obscene' Profits?

Here's where a number of journalists lose their objectivity
—that is the notion of profits. The mindset of these journalists goes
something like this: "Ooooh, companies are out to get profits and
thus they are trying to rip off the consumer and some profits are just
'obscene.'" (The word obscene is often used to describe the profits
of oil companies, but more about that later.) Underlying this mindset is a failure to admit that profits allow stores to stay in business.

If stores didn't make profits, they wouldn't exist and consumers wouldn't be able to buy stuff from them. This might not be
so bad if the store were selling green velour musketeer boots. Consumers could probably do without them.

But what if the store were selling food? It's rather hard to
do without food. They might acknowledge that point, but what if
the price of food goes up? Many journalists immediately blame
the store's greed for more and more profits. A responsible reporter
would look at the causes of the increase—a freeze in Chile, a truck-
ers' strike, a new law that required more employees to fill out reports
to the government—not immediately blame the store's profit motive.

So understanding what a price is and what it does is key to
understanding the world, economically speaking. But how are they
set? Read on, McDuff.

POSSIBLE EXERCISES

• *Discuss how quality is factored into prices.*

• *Discuss how service is factored into prices.*

• *Give examples of products or services that aren't subject to the
usual pressures of price.*

Chapter 2

Setting Prices

D'ya ever wonder why things cost you what they do? Why is a loaf of bread about $2 or a new blouse $40? Some journalists immediately blame the seller for being greedy. If only he weren't so greedy, the journalist "reasons," the price would be lower. To put that notion to rest, all that is required is to ask: "If greed were the answer, why isn't a loaf of bread $10 or $50? And that blouse, why doesn't it cost $100 or $500?" And the simple answer is that no one will pay that price.

Buyers will eat corn meal or wear overalls, which are cheaper, rather than pay those kinds of prices. So sellers have to worry about what consumers will spend for these products. They know that buyers like low prices, not high ones, so they can't go crazy and ask for an arm and a leg for an item or a service. Otherwise, people will look to another store for the product or just do without.

Still, a business exists to make profits. So the quandary that businesses find themselves in is this: how to make the most profits without losing customers. If a journalist understands this quandary, he or she is well on the way to understanding how prices are set.

Alex's Autos

Consider this simple example: You have the ability to make a car, and that car costs $5,000 to build. You'd like to retire early, so you sell your cars for $10,000. That's a 100 percent profit. Life is good and you sell a fair number of cars.

Now, along comes a person who sees that profit margin and

an opportunity. Let's call him Alex Keaton. Alex realizes that he can make a similar car for the same costs—about $5,000. And he decides that he doesn't have to get 100 percent profit. He'd be satisfied with 80 percent, so he sells the car for $9,000. Well, what happens to your customers? Many of them head over to Alex's Autos and pay less.

Then, here comes Tess McGill and she sees the healthy profits in the car business. She too can make a car for about $5,000 and decides to sell her cars for $8,000 for a 60 percent profit. Soon the crowds leave your place and Alex's Autos and head on over to Tess' Transportation.

You and Alex realize that you are losing business, so you get together and agree to sell your respective cars for $7,000. Pretty soon, Tess' showroom is empty while yours and Alex's are hopping. Tess, being a sharp working girl, realizes that she's been the victim of collusion and files a complaint with the government. (Collusion is a secret agreement to do something illegal—in this case, set prices.) But she also lowers her price to $6,000. She figures that the government lawyers will tie your hands for a while, and she's going to cash in.

You and Alex settle with the government and get back to business. You figure that a 20 percent profit is not too bad, so you sell at the same price as Tess. Alex follows suit…for a while. Then, to attract more customers, he sets his price at $5,500, Tess goes to $5,400, you lower to $5,300, and so on. So what started out as one businessman making a killing turned into a fierce competition for customers.

Key to Prices

This competition is key to setting the price of goods. Sellers will sell their products as close as they can to the cost of making that product. If there is no competition, businesses have a greater ability to charge high prices—especially if what they sell is popular or a necessity. In other words, with competion prices are as low as they can get without going below the cost of production.

Now, if a business is the first to introduce a product to a market, that business can expect healthy profits. But those very profits encourage other businesses to get into that market.

That's what happened to Microsoft in the 1980s. It enjoyed the ability to charge pretty high prices for its operating systems and software. It beat out the only other competition, Apple Computer, because Microsoft could charge significantly lower prices than Apple and still reap a plentiful bounty.

But Sun Microsystems, Unix and Linux realized that there was money to be made and they developed operating systems and software that competed with Microsoft. And the result has been lower and lower prices.

Speaking of low prices, d'ya ever wonder how Wal-Mart can sell all those goods at such low prices? It's not as if the shirts and rugs and toys it sells are different from those sold in other stores. How does it do it?

Well, if competition drives prices down toward the cost of production, what does that say about Wal-Mart? It says the executives there have figured out ways to lower the company's cost of production. There's a number of ways they have done this. Buying in bulk, reducing the high costs of inventory, better transportation and distribution systems, and lower employee-related costs all have helped Wal-Mart lower their costs of production. And voila! Lower prices.

Hardware superstores Home Depot and Lowe's followed suit. And Wal-Mart's main competitors, Kmart and Target, have also learned from Wal-Mart and now are able to offer some goods at Wal-Mart prices. But given the motive to make profits, look for Wal-Mart to try to find other ways of lowering their costs of production.

Tiffany Effect

Some businesses do go against these general rules. Take the upscale department store, Neiman Marcus. Their clientele is well-to-do, and the store has determined that their customers are in an income bracket where price is much less of a signal. It's like the old line: If you have to ask how much it costs, you can't afford it. Well, most Neiman Marcus customers don't have to ask. There's also the snob appeal of being able to afford high-priced items that others cannot. Economists call this the Tiffany effect, after the costly (and beautiful) cut-glass lamps Tiffany is famous for.

But in a regular market, prices are a key signal. Businesses, which want high prices, can't afford to lose customers because their prices are higher than other producers. And for consumers, the lower the price, the better. And that's why a loaf of bread costs about $2 and a blouse about $40.

POSSIBLE EXERCISES

- *Track the price of computers and explain the trend.*

- *Define and discuss a "natural monopoly."*

- *Discuss and write about how banks stay in business. What prices do they operate by?*

CHAPTER 3

WHAT AFFECTS PRICES?

So you've got your competitive marketplace. Business rivals look for ways to lower their costs of production so that they can attract more customers with the resulting lower prices. But no marketplace is so pristinely efficient. Things happen beyond the sellers' and buyers' control to raise and lower prices.

Often these price-changing events happen naturally—weather extremes, unrest in a country that provides raw materials, new transportation or delivery options, or an increase in the demand for a product or service. Buyers and sellers adjust accordingly, then. Oil companies, knowing that more people will drive during the summer months, will raise prices. This helps the oil companies explore and drill for more oil to meet the anticipated demand. Similarly, droughts, freezes and floods all can lead to a scarcity of certain materials and sellers have to raise prices. These higher prices discourage some consumers from buying the product and encourage other producers to enter the market.

In the case of scarcity, existing producers may also pursue other methods of obtaining the products. When prices are high, oil companies will develop some oil sources—deep water drilling or oil from tar sands, for instance—whose costs exceeded what was once a competitive price. But at the higher prices, these other methods have become profitable.

Pretty soon, new sources of the product are found, competition begins again and prices fall back down. In some instances of extreme events, such as hurricanes and floods, some products are sold at much higher prices because of the scarcity of that material.

9

Finger-Wagging

What sets many journalists' fingers a-waggin' is that some of these products are basic and cheap or even free during normal times. After almost any hurricane, basic goods such as water, ice, plywood, generators, etc., become scarce. So producers from other parts of the country bring these basic goods to the ravaged area and try to sell them at higher prices. Ice, for example, after Hurricane Andrew in south Florida in 1992 was $8 a bag, or more than four times its usual cost. Plywood was more than twice the usual rate. And, of course, gasoline prices shot up. Indeed, hurricanes in the Gulf of Mexico always boost gas prices because of the fear that supplies will be interrupted, if not ended.

These higher prices send the desired signals. They tell consumers to buy with care or do without, and they tell sellers to produce more in order to reap those higher costs. Some in the media and government call this price gouging. They argue that laws are needed to prevent these producers from making "obscene" profits at the expense of consumers hurting from a disaster (more about this in the next chapter). The media and politicians don't complain, however, when the reverse happens. Nor do consumers.

Say there's a bigger-than-normal crop of wheat one year. This abundance helps force bread prices lower. When there's more bread available, stores have to compete more fiercely for customers. Customers can exert their buying power to keep those prices low. These lower prices then force some producers out of business. And that means less bread comes to market. As supplies of that good become scarcer, prices go up. Some buyers stop buying so much bread, and the failures of bread makers start to slow. Pretty soon, you have buyers and sellers coming to a happy medium. The amount of bread produced is roughly equal to the amount of bread sold at a certain price. Economists call this an equilibrium, or a market-clearing, price.

Government Policies

More than just natural actions can affect prices, though. Government policies of all types can change prices and therefore change the signals they send to buyers. The most obvious way the government affects prices is through taxes. Take the sales tax. There are not too many states where you aren't hit with a 4, 6, 8, even 10 percent extra charge at the cash register. Thus, the price you pay at the register is higher than that listed by the store.

But like all prices, it sends a signal. For example, take the area around Montgomery, Ala. The city charges a 10 percent sales tax. Yet surrounding counties and towns charge 8 percent. So you will hear ads for businesses in those surrounding areas stressing their lower tax rates and therefore lower prices. And consumers end up in nearby Wetumpka or Prattville to shop.

The producer, however, gets signals different from the ones you would expect from higher prices. Even though consumers have to pay more, the businesses don't get that extra income. So other businesses have no real incentive to rush into that business, and existing businesses have to make profits similar to competitors outside Montgomery but with fewer customers because of the high prices.

It's no surprise, then, that a 726,883 square-foot mall in Montgomery lost shoppers and tenants so that by the time it was sold in May 2007 it had just a handful of tenants (many of them transient). It wasn't just pricing that did in Montgomery Mall. It was located in an area that had seen its residents go from middle- to upper middle class to a lower-middle and lower income demographic. Crime there increased, as did competition from more upscale malls across town in a higher-income area. But the taxes didn't help.

Another way to gauge the effect of taxes is to look at so-called capital gains taxes. This essentially is a tax on the increase in value of investments such as stocks and bonds, real estate, art work, etc. This tax is only imposed when the sale is made and the gain is realized. So if the tax rates are too high, investors will not sell their gains—in other words, they're not willing to pay the high price represented by the tax rate. But if the tax rate falls, investors face a lower price and are much more likely to sell their investment and realize their gain.

You may be muttering to yourself: But if I made a big gain on my investment, why wouldn't I want to sell it so I could have some more money to spend? The answer is that as your gain goes up, so does the amount of taxes you pay. The higher the rate, the more you pay as your investment grows in value.

For a simplified example, let's assume you've been savvy in an investment and made $10,000 over what you originally paid for it. The capital gains tax is 20 percent. So you would owe $2,000 in taxes, leaving only $8,000 in your pocket from the sale. But you hear that Congress is talking about reducing that rate. It does, and now the rate is 15 percent. When you realize your gain, you'll have $8,500. Don't you think you'd wait till the tax rate went down? In other words, you would wait until the price of doing something dropped.

In fact, that's exactly what happened after Congress in 2003 dropped the capital gains rate from 20 percent to 15 percent. "According to early tabulations from 2004 tax returns, capital gains realizations grew by about 50 percent in 2004," reported the Congressional Budget Office. In short, a year after capital gains tax rates went down, sales of investments increased by 50 percent. And this principle applies to whatever the government taxes. Income, corporate profits, different goods and services. The higher the tax rate, the fewer "buyers" you'll have. In this case, the buyers are citizens who decide to engage in the activity or buy the good that is taxed.

For the most part, taxes are a visible way the government affects prices. A less noticeable method of influencing prices is through subsidies.

Education Assistance

Take education assistance. The government subsidizes the cost of college education through grants and loans. You may even have one. That makes the cost of college cheaper for individuals. That indeed was the express purpose of passing student aid programs. And that lower price encourages people to seek a college education. And the lower price has had its effect. In 1972, the year Pell grants were established, college enrollment was 49.2 percent. Less than half of high school graduates enrolled in college. By 2004, that number had increased to 66.7 percent.

Other factors were in play, as well, mainly the growth of the number of people in the 16-to-24 age group. They were children of the baby boomer generation. But the lower price associated with going to college certainly helped spur the growth in enrollment.

Another less visible way government action can affect prices is through regulations. These are the rules that businesses have to follow in order to comply with state and federal laws. Reporting on the diversity of the workforce, continual monitoring of pollution control efforts, and ensuring that every transaction is accounted for are all regulations that face many businesses. But these activities aren't free. It takes people to keep records and report to the government. These people have to be paid, but little of the spending on these people helps the business produce the goods it sells. So it's a cost of production that has to be reflected in the price of the good or service being sold.

Costly Rules

And it is costly. According to an estimate by economists with the Competitive Enterprise Institute, it cost businesses more than $1 trillion in 2006 to comply with regulation. Considering that the gross domestic product was $13 trillion in 2006, regulatory costs were almost 8 percent of the total output of the economy in the United States.

While not all regulatory costs are passed along in the form of higher prices, economists agree that much of these costs are passed on. And what happens when prices are high? Consumers don't buy as much. It's not too much of a stretch to say, then, that if the cost of regulation rises too high, it could have a real effect on consumers' buying habits, which are a big part of the economy.

The best example of this is the oil industry. Some of the

regulations that the industry faces include:

- Requirements to blend gases differently for different regions of the country;
- Stringent pollution controls that have prevented companies from building any new refineries since 1977; and
- Bans on drilling both on-shore (Alaska and much of the West) and off-shore (Florida and California).

All these regulations have made gasoline more scarce and helped put an upward pressure on prices. Here's how a report by the Congressional Research Service of the Library of Congress put it in 2006: "In addition to higher petroleum prices there were forces —some of which were understood (factors such as environmental regulations and pipeline breaks) and others that are still are not so clearly understood—that caused the prices of refined petroleum products to spike."

In an earlier report, CRS estimated that 24 to 30 cents of a gas spike in 2000 could be attributed to the cost of new regulations on gasoline formulas, This is not an argument for removing regulations from the oil industry, just an observation that regulations can boost prices. Unfortunately, reporters rarely look at regulations as a part of the price of gas. Rather, they focus on the profits the oil companies are making or the "greedy" actions of a gas station owner.

But while the desire for profits motivates all businesses, including the oil industry, high prices aren't usually the result of unchecked greed on the part of business. Rather, outside forces, including government policies, are the culprit behind high prices.

Finally, there is one other way that government affects prices and that's through inflation. But because money is a government creation, there isn't a working market with competitors for the ability to create money. For further discussion, see Appendix I.

But as you can see, the government has many ways to affect prices indirectly through taxes and subsidies. Government, though, can take an even more direct role in affecting prices and that's the subject of the next chapter.

POSSIBLE EXERCISES

- *Discuss why federal revenues from income taxes grew after those tax rates were cut.*

- *Break down the cost of a gallon of gasoline.*

- *Predict the pricing trends of a technological break through.*

CHAPTER 4

FIXING PRICES

Because everyone (read that as every voter) doesn't like to pay a lot for, well, anything, politicians often feel they can appeal to voters by tinkering with high prices. But politicians also have political donors who fund their campaigns. Those donors would like high prices and can be very persuasive. If those donors are in a particular business, they urge politicians to step in and try to boost the prices the donors' companies will get for their goods and services. The politicians want to keep their donors happy so they try to pass laws that require higher prices for those goods.

The media, especially when it comes to tinkering with high prices, often write uncritical stories of these efforts to "control" prices. The tenor of these stories usually goes something like this: "Government has finally taken action to put a stop to skyrocketing prices of (fill in the blank)." But what the media usually fail to report is the effect of these efforts. And those effects are obvious, even predictable, for journalists who understand what prices are and what they do.

Deals on Wheels

Again, consider a simple example. You're in a college town, and you realize that there is no good place to buy a decent bicycle. So you get some money together (loans, the parents, investors, whatever) and you open up Deals on Wheels. But business at first is slow. So you figure you'll bring in customers with a sale. You look at your books and you make some tough decisions. You pay $100 for a bike from the manufacturer, and you sell it for $110. But without customers, you realize that you need to do something.

So you decide to sell some bicycles for $80 as a way to draw customers to Deals on Wheels. You know that you can't continue to sell your bikes at a loss, so you say it's a one-day only sale. And sure enough, the word gets out, and you've got more customers than you can handle. They can't fit in the store and spill out on the street. Little did you know that a lawmaker passed by, saw the crowd and realized something good was going on.

The politician goes back to Washington, D.C., and convinces his colleagues that an $80 bicycle is a great thing. "Bicycles have so many benefits," intones the lawmaker. "They can help you get healthy. And the more people who ride bikes, the less pollution there is. And, of course, more people riding bicycles will help the United States become less dependent on foreign oil."

To thunderous applause, the politician sits down and watches his bill that will cap the price of bicycles at $80 pass in a near unanimous vote. (The politician and all his colleagues have calculated that a lot of votes will come their way in the next election as a result of this bill).

But for you, the one-day sale has become a permanent condition. You can't find bicycles for less than $90, so you're going to be selling all bikes in your shop at a loss.

Do you stay in business? Is the bear a Catholic?

You instead sell off the rest of your inventory and explore other employment opportunities. You've heard that other bike sellers were doing the same thing. Meanwhile, the customers are still clamoring for cheap bicycles.

Then the media weighs in: A critical shortage of bicycles has government and private sector analysts perplexed. "It seemed to happen overnight," said Robert Brunnez, a legislative assistant to committee Chairman Joseph Harrison Payne. "I'm not sure what happened," said Anita Angstrom, a policy analyst for the Energy Alternatives Foundation.

One expert questioned the bicycle industry's motives. "I think they're holding ships offshore, filled with bikes, in order to bring a lot of pressure on the legislature," said Con Spearasee of the Destiny Group.

Far-fetched? A little. But it's reflective of the piddling amount of common sense, not to mention economic sense, found in the media and government.

Now jump forward a couple of months. The media has kept up a constant stream of stories about the "bicycle crisis." Bicycle manufacturers have marched on the capital, demanding assistance. And the public is writing letters to the legislature complaining about the lack of bicycles. Now politicians realize that their good (and vote-seeking) intentions may have gone awry.

Relief?

So they proudly announce that they've passed the "Bicycle Sellers Relief Act." And in that law, the legislature required that all bicycles be sold at $200. And if the sellers couldn't find any in the public willing to pay $200, then the government would buy the bikes, using a complicated set of bike price supports.

Well, you see that and say, "Hey, there's money to be made now. I'm back in business." You take out a second mortgage on your house and you buy as many bicycles as you can for $100. So who cares if nobody buys a bike? The government will take them off your hands.

Then you discover that your best friend is doing the same thing, and the guy down the street has closed his garage and gone into the bike business. Your mother also calls you with questions about where you can buy $100 bikes. What does it matter if you have all these competitors? The government will make sure all of them stay in business, so they're not really rivals.

Pretty soon, though, the government's budget is bleeding red ink. Debt is piling up and so are bicycles in government warehouses.

The media weighs in again. The bicycle crisis has apparently been solved, while the future of the mom-and-pop bicycle shop seems secure. "I can't believe what a burden has been lifted from my shoulders," said (your mom's name here). "My retirement is secure."

Amid the relief, though, the specter of mounting deficits haunts lawmakers as they struggle to find ways to pay for the bicycle relief act.

"We don't want to raise taxes," said committee Chairman Joseph Harrison Payne. "But not only are the cost of price supports increasing more rapidly than we projected, but the costs to store the surplus bicycles are soaring, as well."

It's easy to see the results of these efforts to control prices, but journalists rarely pay much attention to these efforts. They should, however, by remembering two simple statements. When prices are fixed by law below what it costs to produce something, there is a shortage. On the other hand, if the price is fixed by law above what it costs to make something, you'll get a surplus.

Let's go back to bicycles. Lawmakers realize they may have gone too far in setting the bicycle price so high. So they pass a law reducing the mandated price to $180. And some people, exhibiting the Tiffany effect, buy a bicycle or two. Meanwhile, one or two sellers see that their guaranteed profits have gone down, so they get out of the bike business, looking for other sure-fire opportunities.

Still, the government is buying up bikes at a rapid rate and costs are soaring. So lawmakers pass another law that lowers the fixed price to $160. A few more buyers are willing to pay that price and a few more sellers get out.

So now you ask: Why doesn't the government just do away with the price supports? The reason for that is that bicycle sellers have banded together to lobby for continuing the price supports. (They have some extra money, right?) The sellers convince lawmakers that it's in the national interest to keep bicycle sellers in business and that it's in the interest of lawmakers to support the bike sellers, as the bike sellers are big contributors to friendly lawmakers' campaign chests.

But lawmakers also have to worry about their constituents, so they pass a law that sets the price near the market-clearing price of $11. Then they also pass a law that mandates higher prices for certain bike sellers (especially ones from heavily populated states). So a complex set of price rules are developed to reward favored producers. Consumers are quieted, some bike sellers are happy and the lawmakers feel a little better about holding on to their seats (See Chapter 14).

Of course, taxpayers have to pick up the tab for the remaining bicycle price support payments. All because government started tinkering with prices. Unfortunately, too many reporters don't understand the effects of price fixing by government, and therefore fail to inform the public of what's really happening.

What? You say that it's so obvious, how could government be fixing prices? Don't lawmakers know what kind of disruptions these price controls produce? Judging from today's society, you'd have to answer that no, lawmakers aren't aware of these disruptions. And if they are aware, they choose to ignore the results, usually for political reasons. That becomes clearer when you start looking at different parts of the economy, which is what the rest of this book is about.

POSSIBLE EXERCISES

- *Give as many examples as you can of goods or services not subject to price controls.*

- *Find three historical examples of price controls.*

- *Discuss the ability of businesses to fix prices. Define collusion.*

CHAPTER 5

HEALTH CARE

"Health care is too important to leave to the market." Politicians make this argument all the time. Consider the words of 2008 presidential candidate, John Edwards. In a plan he said would provide health care to everyone, Edwards said, "Everyone will belong to a health care market, which will be set up by government." And the media dutifully report these kinds of pronouncements without question or analysis.

Behind these pronouncements is a belief that patients and doctors shouldn't have to worry about prices—a belief that talking about money when you go to the doctor is crass and secondary to the mission of curing disease and treating injury.

The appeal of this argument has led the government and the private sector to impose a range of price controls that have had predictable results. Predictable at least to any journalist who understands how prices work.

To see what's happening in the health care field, it's necessary to go back to the 1940s. It was war time and the government had assumed a great deal of control over the economy. There was rationing of all sorts of goods, such as gasoline and rubber, aluminum foil and sugar. And with tight supplies came high prices, so the federal government also put limits on prices of such goods and services, including the price of workers, i.e., their salaries. Because companies couldn't use higher salaries to attract workers, they sought other attractions.

One such was offering health care to employees in the guise of "prepaid service plans." The hospitals argued that this health care was a business expense and the Internal Revenue Service eventually agreed with that argument. This position was eventually expanded to include the cost of health insurance. This meant that companies could buy health insurance for their workers and deduct it from their income taxes. (This was key to health care problems today.) The IRS also determined that the workers would not be taxed on the value of the health insurance.

By the time wage controls were ended in 1946, more than 14 percent of Americans had health coverage that cost them little and prompted no taxation. Typically, health insurance or "prepaid" plans would cover most medical procedures in exchange for a monthly premium. Thus, there was really no price the consumer had to pay when he or she used medical services. It was effectively zero. So what happens when a consumer doesn't have to pay for a good or service?

Luxury Cars

For the answer, ask yourself what you would do if someone gave you a no-limit credit card and you didn't have to pay off the debt. How about buying an island or 17 luxury cars or an evening in Paris with your favorite celebrity? It's not really your money, so you don't care what you spend.

The same thing happened in the health care field. Patients didn't have to pay for the health care they got (maybe a small deductible), so they wanted as much as they could get. Hang nails were worth a doctor's visit. So too were sniffles and bruises. The doctors and hospitals were getting paid, so they didn't care how much health care they delivered, even if it wasn't really needed. Both the patient and the provider were thus shielded from how much the service cost and the signals they received led to a greater and greater demand for health care.

And, boy, was it popular. Some 130 million Americans had health insurance in 1960, representing about 87 percent of the population. Yet, only about half of Americans aged 65 or older had health insurance in 1965. That's because insurance companies knew that older people were more likely to need health care. So much so that the premiums from healthy workers couldn't cover the costs of the less healthy seniors.

Medicare

So in 1965, the Democratically controlled Congress, led by President Lyndon Johnson, passed the Medicare program, which set up a government health plan for the elderly. Modeled after the Social Security program, Medicare was designed to provide free health care to the nation's senior citizens. It would be financed with a small deduction from every worker's pay check and every person aged 65 and older would get their health care for basically nothing. And while this was a political masterstroke [1], it was an economic problem waiting to happen. Why? Because lawmakers ignored or dismissed the effects of setting a price for a service below what it costs to provide that service.

Remember the bicycle example? A price control on bicycles below the cost of production signaled to consumers to buy cheap bikes. But it also told producers that they couldn't make any money. And when you have high demand and low supply, you get a shortage. And that's where the Medicare program stands today—waiting lists, fewer doctors who see Medicare patients and shorter hospital stays are all evidence of a shortage in medical care for senior citizens.

In the original Medicare plan, doctors and hospitals were paid their "usual, customary and reasonable" costs. So doctors got paid, patients got free health care and everyone was happy—everyone, that is, except taxpayers. In 1967, the first year Medicare was fully in effect, spending was a little more than $3 billion. And policymakers predicted that costs would reach $12 billion by 1990. It's as if that six-pack of soda that cost $2 went up to $8. But you wouldn't care. You weren't paying for it.

As it happens, the Medicare system saw double-digit percentage increases in spending every year, but two, from 1966 to 1990. The actual cost of Medicare in 1990 was more than $98 billion. In soda pop terms, that six-pack now cost $93. But again, why should you care?

Indeed, the trustees of the Medicare trust fund in 1970 said that the fund would be insolvent in two years because costs far exceeded the revenues. So, in order to pay these soaring costs, taxes were raised.

In 1966, the payroll tax was 0.35 percent of income. By 1990, that figure had gone up to 1.45 percent, a fourfold increase. In 1983, Medicare costs had risen to almost $57 billion and the red ink was piling up. Because of these higher costs, lawmakers were faced with the choice of voting for even higher taxes or cutting benefits.

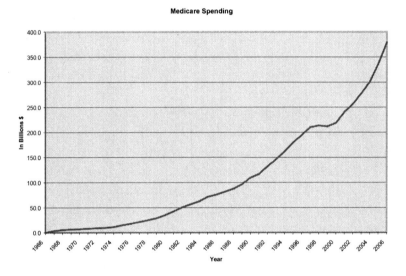

Medicare Spending

Source: U.S. Office of Management and Budget, 2006

A third option of revamping the whole system to make consumers and producers more aware of prices was dismissed. Why? Because the opposing political party scored many political points by saying that its rivals wanted to do away with free health care for seniors. And, remember, seniors vote. So none of these options was a winning political strategy.

Lawmakers, then, deliberated awhile, slapped their forehead and said: "Eureka, price controls! Why didn't we think of them sooner? We can require low prices. That'll be an easy sell, politically. We'll show fiscal discipline while still giving away services. What a deal!"

It might have been a good deal for politicians, but not for doctors. Rather than getting reimbursed for their costs plus some extra compensation, doctors and hospitals now were getting less than what it cost to provide their services. Of course, politicians didn't call their actions on Medicare price controls. They instead called their plan a prospective payment system and they came up with the bureaucratic sounding Diagnostic-Related Groups.

Under the DRG system, prices for almost every medical procedure are assigned a reimbursement rate—a price control, by any other name. Of course, not all hospitals face the same costs. City hospitals have higher costs of living to deal with. Teaching hospitals have more staff to pay. Rural hospitals have to pay more for professionals to attract them.

All of these factors were included in the price control calculation, so that today's system is a muddled mess that requires accountants, attorneys and statisticians to decipher.

But a price control is a price control. And these price controls are by and large set below what it costs all these hospitals to provide the services. According to the Health and Human Services Department, Medicare reimbursement rates are about 80 percent of private reimbursement rates.

Another to way to look at it is found in the growth of costs vs. reimbursements. According to Medicare, costs for rural hospitals rose an average annual rate of 6.2 percent. But average annual Medicare payments rose 4.7 percent. It was even worse for urban hospitals. Costs rose 6.2 percent a year while payments only increased 2.7 percent a year.

Predictably, shortages in health care for the elderly have popped up throughout the system. For instance, according to a survey conducted by the Medicare system in 2006, some 3.3 percent of doctors did not accept any Medicare patients. That's compared to 1.7 percent of doctors who did not accept privately insured, non-HMO patients.

Also, the growth in the patient discharge rate was higher than the rate for all payers. That means the number of Medicare patients being discharged was growing more rapidly than the number of all patients being sent home. If you remove Medicare patients from the all-patients category, then the Medicare discharge rate is significantly greater than all other patients.

Even more indicative of shortages in the Medicare system has to do with the average length of hospital stays. According to the Medicare system, a decrease in the length of stay for Medicare patients dropped more rapidly than for all patients. In 2005, for instance, the number of days in the hospital for Medicare patients dropped by about 8 percent. For all patients, the number of days in the hospital dropped less than 2 percent.

What this means is that Medicare patients were getting kicked out of hospitals at a faster rate than all patients put together. And since all patients include Medicare patients, non-Medicare patients were able to stay even longer in hospitals.

Medicaid

This rationing of health care is by no means limited to the Medicare system. The government's program for the low-income population, Medicaid, is even worse.

Because reimbursement rates are even lower than those of Medicare, the shortages are even more pronounced. For example, almost 30 percent of doctors would not take Medicaid patients in 2006. And half of all the doctors who accepted Medicaid patients said finding a referral for these patients was "very difficult."

Further aggravating the problems in the Medicaid system is the fact that it is a joint program between the federal government and the states. And states determine how much they will spend on Medicaid. For instance, Alabama and Connecticut have roughly the same amount of people, but they differ widely in their Medicaid spending. In 2004, Alabama spent $1.42 billion while Connecticut spent $3.54 billion.

Other states have restructured their Medicaid systems with

predictable results. Take Tennessee. In 1993, the state received permission from the Clinton administration to expand their Medicaid system to cover more citizens. But state policymakers decreed that these new patients would pay little for their care. And because there were no accurate price signals, patients demanded, doctors provided and spending skyrocketed under the so-called TennCare program.

Because of this cost surge, then-Republican Gov. Don Sundquist proposed the state's first income tax. This proposal led to a tax revolt where thousands of Tennesseans besieged the state capitol, forcing legislators to abandon their plans to install an income tax. TennCare spending, though, continued to balloon, so that by 2005, Democratic Gov. Phil Bredesen was forced to cut more than 320,000 adults from the rolls. That's the ultimate form of rationing —total denial of care. Still more than a fourth of Tennessee's population gets Tenncare benefits.

Other states, however, have begun to take the pricing mechanism into account in their reforms of Medicaid. In South Carolina, a test program would give beneficiaries a personal health account that would be funded by the state. With the money in this account, beneficiaries can choose among several state-approved plans. The choices include an option to buy a catastrophic insurance plan and use the rest of the fund to pay for other medical services as needed. While this still insulates beneficiaries from price signals, this program will probably lead to less rationing, as low-income consumers have more control over their health choices.

Speaking of choices, do working adults get much choice in their health care coverage? According to the Employee Benefits Research Institute, only about half of all workers can choose among several health insurance plans.

HMO Sap-iens

Of the 88 percent of firms who offered health insurance in 2006, just 7 percent offered conventional health insurance plans – that is, an insurance company pays for services rendered. [2] In 2006, some 17 percent offered health maintenance organization coverage,

54 percent offered preferred provider organization plans and 22 percent offered point-of-service plans.

The main characteristic of each of these types of plans is an attempt to control insurance company spending by limiting health options. Economists have a word for this. It's called rationing.

HMOs require consumers to go to one provider—usually a collection of doctors—and receive whatever care is provided. Unfortunately for the patient, the way an HMO makes any money is by skimping on care. Doctor visits are shorter, referrals are fewer in number and amenities are in short supply.

PPOs provide a little more flexibility to patients, but the method's incentives still limit care. A patient chooses a doctor among a list of preferred providers, but may go elsewhere. However, if a patient goes outside the PPO network, the cost of deductibles and so-called co-payments goes up.

In a POS plan, patients choose a primary provider, but must pay almost all the costs of services provided by someone other than that primary doctor.

In all these plans, health care is rationed to one degree or another. More specifically, insurance companies make decisions that deny care. The reason for all this denial of care is obvious to the journalist conversant in the area of prices and their function. Because the actual price of buying and providing a service is not apparent to the consumer and the producer, the signals each get conflict wildly.

Patients want more care because the price is so low, while producers want to provide less care because they aren't being fully reimbursed. Thus, you have a shortage of health care.

(1) Politicians like to give things to voters (See Chapter 14). And because seniors vote in greater numbers than any other age group, giving away free health care was surefire way to appeal to these voters.

(2) Employee Benefits Research Institute, "Sources of Health Insurance and Characteristics of the Uninsured," May 2007.

POSSIBLE EXERCISES

- *Investigate another country's health care system – particularly those that offer universal coverage. What happens to prices in those systems?*

- *Investigate the veterans health care system. What happens to price in that system? Do they provide adequate medical coverage for all?*

- *Write a story about a local hospital's payments and costs.*

- *Describe and discuss the process of bringing a prescription drug to market.*

CHAPTER 6

ENERGY

What do gas shortages, rolling blackouts and soaring food prices have in common—besides the fact that they are all bad news? They are all the result of government efforts to tinker with energy prices. No, this is not some conspiracy theory, involving sacks of cash, black helicopters or an invasion by the mutants of Alpha Centauri. Rather, it is what a savvy journalist discovers when looking at the energy pricing mechanism.

And that journalist doesn't have far to look. Government has intruded on energy pricing more than most others. Why? Because virtually every voter must purchase energy, whether gasoline or electricity. And when prices of those commodities bother consumers—who want things for free, after all—the government usually steps in. And usually the government makes it worse.

Take shortages. (Remember that shortages are different from scarcity.) Gasoline shortages hit American drivers at the beginning and end of the 1970s. Not because there wasn't enough gas, but rather because the government had put price controls on it. These shortages were evident in long lines at the gas pump and in odd-even rationing schemes that depended on your license plate number.

Let's take a look at the marketplace for oil in 1973. According to the Energy Department, domestic oil was selling for $4.17 a barrel. That translated into a per-gallon cost of 34 cents. Meanwhile, imported crude oil cost $4.08 a barrel, and it helped keep the supply and demand for gasoline in roughly equal amounts. In other words, the price controls in place in 1973 didn't have a lot of effect.

But in 1974, domestic crude oil jumped by almost 75 percent

to $7.18 a barrel, while crude oil imports saw a jump of more than 300 percent to $12.52 a barrel. But President Nixon's complex price control system only allowed prices at the pump to rise by 55 percent. And you had gas lines, such as the one pictured below.

Typical of the coverage of this shortage was a TV reporter who would go to motorists in a gas line, shove a microphone in their faces and come up with hard-hitting questions.

"How do you feel about waiting in line for gas?" asked the reporter.

"How do you think? This really stinks. And I'm getting pretty (BEEP) off."

Or you might have heard this exchange.

Oil Company Villains?

"Who do you think is responsible for this shortage?"

"Oh, man. It's the oil companies. A friend of mine who's a deep-sea fisherman said he saw dozens of oil company ships just waiting out of sight of land. And he said they were riding real low in the water. So I figure those damn oil companies are just hoarding oil until the price goes up."

Through the mid-1970s, crude oil prices stabilized and only rose gradually. The price controls kept pretty close to that increase. That is, until 1979. Then domestic crude oil prices rose some 40 percent, while imported oil rose near 50 percent. But the price was only allowed to increase by about 30 percent. And the result was quick and easy to predict.

Some analysts suggest that these gas lines were a big reason for President Carter's loss in 1980 to Ronald Reagan. Reagan, as president, had an intuitive understanding of what happens when government tries to monkey with prices.

In 1982, he had removed all price controls on gasoline. His critics in Congress and the media predicted that gas prices would skyrocket, plunging the economy into recession. But rather than increasing, or even staying flat, gas prices actually fell. This, after 10 straight years of gas price increases—mandated under a price control system. Reagan removed the system and poof! High gas prices disappeared, as did gas lines and all rationing schemes.

Gas Prices

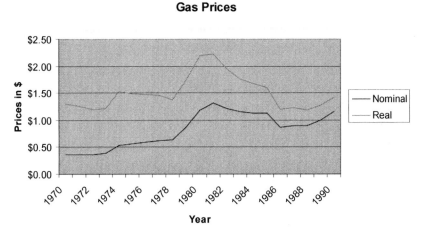

Sources: Platt's Oil Price Handbook and Oilmanac, 1974, 51st ed.,
Energy Information Administration (EIA), annual averages of monthly data from the U.S. Department of Labor, Bureau of Labor Statistics

After the country's experience with energy price controls, it would seem reasonable to assume that politicians wouldn't try them again.

Not so fast, my friend. They could, and they did.

To be fair, politicians have refrained from trying to tinker with gasoline price controls again. But when it comes to other sources of energy, the lessons of the 1970s have been lost on policy makers.

California Scheming

In California, for instance, the state government started getting complaints from electricity customers who had seen their utility bills start to soar. More demand pushed these prices higher, but so did a complicated electricity market, run by the state, that ensured wholesale energy prices would be high. But at the same time, California law had price controls on the retail price of electricity, i.e., your lights, your computer, your automatic garage door opener.

Then-Gov. Gray Davis said it was the power companies' fault, and the federal government's, and the gluttonous appetite of the high-tech industry for more energy. He couldn't blame the politicians, because he was one of the politicians who helped pass the law that created the problem. So Davis refused to lift the price controls, and rolling blackouts hit the state in the summer of 2001. His answer to the problem of energy shortages? Guarantee high prices in long-term contracts to energy producers so they would keep supplies up, and therefore prices down.

In shorthand, to solve the problem of shortages caused by price controls, he installed price controls that created a surplus. And guess who had to pay for this surplus? California taxpayers. The state had to borrow $50 billion in the municipal bond market to make these deals, thus adding to the state's debt.

If Davis had removed the state from the energy market, retail prices would have spiked for a while. And ratepayers would have still been ticked. But these higher prices would have encouraged ratepayers to conserve on their use of electricity ("How many times do I have to tell you to turn that light off when you leave a room?"). Plus, the higher prices would have attracted other energy producers to enter the market, thereby increasing the supply of electricity. And this competition would have inevitably led to lower prices for the retail customer.

A Gallon of Corn?

Low prices are also not in the picture for consumers of another commodity, as a result of government monkeying with prices. That commodity? Food. Huh? Energy price controls lead to higher food prices? How does that work?

To get a picture of that, it's necessary first to look at the energy program and then its effect on food prices. The energy program involves ethanol, an alcohol-based fuel derived from plants. And the government is very much involved in the ethanol market and has been since the late 1970s.

In the ethanol program, though, the government does not impose a straight price control. Instead, the government offers a substantial tax break to ethanol producers. This tax break acts like a price control set above the cost of production because it guarantees a price over what buyers would spend for corn, which is what most ethanol is made from.

Look at it this way. A corn processor pays taxes on the profit it makes from selling corn. If it can reduce the amount of taxes it pays, it gets to keep more of its profit. So, if a processor sells corn for use as food or feed, the processor has to pay more in taxes. But if he sells corn for use as ethanol, he pockets more of his profit because of the tax break. In addition, the government has required that 15 percent of all motor fuel be made from renewable sources by 2012. So, the government has essentially guaranteed this higher profit.

Remember the Bicycle Relief Act? You would have taken out a second mortgage to get in on the action of selling bicycles for a big profit. Well, that's what corn processors have done. In 2000, there were 54 ethanol plants in this country. In 2007, that number had swelled to 119. Ethanol production more than doubled, as well. This means that less corn is going to the food and feed markets. And the corn that is going there approaches prices that return the same level of profits that the ethanol corn generates.

Indeed, spending on food in the United States rose 6.6 percent from 2005 to 2006 and, in 2007 "(a)s high corn prices have increased, producer feed costs, beef, pork, and poultry price increases have accelerated," said the U.S. Department of Agriculture.

Of course, none of this argues for or against ethanol use. Renewable fuels would seem a good way out of a dependence on oil. But informed journalists should be able to report that the ethanol price mechanism has certain, predictable outcomes.

POSSIBLE EXERCISES

• *Write a story about the findings of government studies on so-called gas-gouging.*

• *Write a story about what's happened to candy and cola makers.*

• *Compare gasoline prices in the United States and Europe. What is the reason for the differences?*

• *Write a story about how a local gas station sets its prices.*

• *What other federal policies may have an effect on energy prices?*

• *Hybrid vehicles – do they enjoy any subsidies from the government? If so, describe them.*

CHAPTER 7

EDUCATION

Most media discussion of education issues usually focuses on topics such as curriculum, teacher salaries and school prayer. Rarely do reporters look at the economics of the public school system. But fear not, this chapter will do just that.

One of the chief attributes of the public school system is that it's free. Yes, families usually have to pay for lunches and extracurricular activities, but the main product of schools—teaching services—is free.

But is it?

Looking at it another way, students pay nothing or zero for the service. And what does a low price do? It encourages the use of it, just as it did in the health care field. In fact, the free price is required by law, thus making it a price control. And since teachers have to be paid, buildings have to be built and heated, and supplies must be bought, the cost of production of teaching services obviously exceeds the price allowed under law.

So the government, rather than students, pays for these items. But, just as in the health care field, government pockets are not bottomless. Lawmakers have to make choices about what to spend and what to spend it on. And despite the public and political support for education, the government cannot pay for everything education consumers demand. So policymakers put a price control on education and its components. And the informed journalist knows what such a price control leads to: shortages.

Consider the average scores of college-bound seniors from 1966 to 2004. In the verbal section of the test in 2004, average scores

39

dropped by almost 6.5 percent.

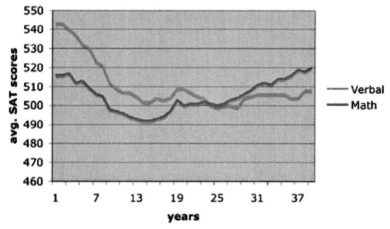

Soure: College Board

In the math section, scores dipped by about 4.5 percent, then gradually rose back to 1966 levels.

Another indicator of a shortage in quality education is the number of schools that offer college-level and advanced placement courses. About seven in 10 fall into those categories. That means at almost a third of the public high schools in the country, students do not have access to higher levels of instruction.

Education shortages show up in other areas, ranging from teaching to textbooks to buildings. Take teachers, for instance. The shortage is so pronounced that the Department of Education publishes an annual list of teacher shortages in all 50 states. And only seven states did not report any shortages in the 2006-07 school year.

Here are some of the areas where teachers are in short supply: English, math, social studies, physical science, language arts, music, art, special education, reading and elementary education. (All of which raises the question: How are children learning anything? This speaks to the dedication and hard work of the remaining teachers.)

That's what happens when the price paid is lower than the cost of production. In this case, the production costs of a teacher can be gauged by the comparability of pay with other professions. And as it is lower than many that require the same amount of training, many teachers and would-be teachers decide to do something else. Law can also mandate an increase in the cost of production, and this means even greater shortages.

No Teacher Left?

Again, looking at teachers, consider the No Child Left Behind Act. Its aim was to increase the quality of education by imposing standards of achievement AND standards of quality for teachers. Tens of thousands of teachers across the country could not meet these higher quality standards, at least not without going back to school. And as tuition isn't free, teachers had the choice of spending money to stay employed in their profession, or leaving the profession and possibly earning more money. And…poof, instant shortage.

But it's not just teachers that are in short supply in the education field. Consider this from a survey conducted by the National Education Association in 2002. "One out of six elementary and secondary school teachers who use textbooks in their classes say they do not have enough books for every child in their class, and nearly one in three teachers report they do not have enough textbooks so that all students can take a textbook home."

Here, too, is evidence of a price control at work, but in a slightly different way. Students have to pay nothing for textbooks. This low price doesn't necessarily increase demand, though. Rather, because none of the students' or the parents' money is tied up in the textbook, the incentive to protect and preserve the good is absent, or at least much diminished. In other words, since they don't own it, they don't take care of it. So losing it is no big deal.

And these shortages show up in school districts from California to South Carolina. One school district in Columbus, Georgia, had a shortage in 2006, but didn't even know how severe it was until the Columbus Ledger-Enquirer asked about it. More than 8 percent of students didn't have a book when the school year started. The Columbus City Council authorized the extra funds needed to buy more textbooks, but the fact there was a shortage in the first place can be traced to a low price imposed by government law.

No Class

Another way shortages crop up in education is in classroom space. The Department of Education conducted a survey in 1999 of the amount of overcrowding in school around the country and found that more than one in five schools had enrollments that were at least 6 percent over the designed capacity.

Some may argue that the fact that the remaining 78 percent of schools were not overcrowded undercuts the theory of shortage-inducing price controls. But what about the schools which are bursting at the seams? Is their shortage of classroom space a product of magic or sunspots or the dog that eats students' homework? Not hardly. They are mostly a result of the price controls on education.

Finally, while there is little data on shortages in school supplies, anecdotes from parents suggest that families and neighborhoods do a lot of fund-raising to buy, or just provide, such items as construction paper, markers, chalk, pencils, playground balls and equipment, to name a few items.

One attempt to avoid the effects of education price controls can be found in a controversial program known variously as school vouchers, school choice, subsidized private education or tuition tax credits. Adopted fully in just two cities, Milwaukee and Cleveland, this approach provides money to low-income parents to pay for tuition at private schools. Parents can choose among a number of schools and specialties. Typically, though, the subsidy does not cover the full tuition costs. So parents have to put up some of their own money. The result is that prices are more apparent to consumers and providers and therefore send more appropriate signals. If the consumer is not satisfied with the product or the price paid, he or she can go to another provider. So providers have a real motivation to provide satisfactory service. And judging by some of the research on these programs, not only is the service satisfactory, it's better than those offered by public schools.

Studies of the program in Milwaukee, which has been in place the longest, have shown that voucher students graduated at a higher rate and had higher test scores than similar students in the public schools. A review by Jay Greene of the Manhattan Institute for Policy Research, for instance, showed that almost two-thirds of voucher students who entered school in 1999 graduated in 2003. That's compared to 41 percent from public schools with selective admission requirements and 34 percent in other Milwaukee public schools.

Interestingly, the teachers unions, which oppose such voucher programs, were successful in blocking any assessments by the state or city after 2000. It's easy to see why. If the voucher program is providing more quality in education, and more students choose to participate, public schools stand to lose lots of money because they'd get fewer students. Cleveland has shown similar results.

One result of these programs is improvement in the public schools themselves. Just like the competing car dealers, schools there are competing for customers. Ironically, because the state government cannot afford vouchers for every student who wants one, it has to set a limit on the number of vouchers. So a shortage of quality education remains. Still, the success of the choice system has meant more jurisdictions going along. Here's a report from the Heritage Foundation, a right-of-center research group in Washington, D.C.:

• "As of April 2005, students in six states—Florida, Maine, Ohio, Vermont, Utah, and Wisconsin—and the District of Columbia can receive government-funded scholarships to attend a private school of choice.

•"Six states—Arizona, Florida, Illinois, Iowa, Minnesota, and Pennsylvania—offer tax credits or deductions for education expenses or contributions to scholarship programs."

The most important feature of all these programs is bringing a consciousness to price back into the educational system. And while continuing caps and rules—backed, of course, by teacher unions—try to limit choice programs, the record shows that when consumers and providers are sensitive to price, the resulting competition leads to more satisfied customers.

POSSIBLE EXERCISES

- *Do a story on your local high school. Are there any shortages there? In what?*

- *Describe the different ways lawmakers have tried to introduce price into the education field.*

- *How many states and localities have tried to introduce price into education? Do a story.*

CHAPTER 8

CRIME

For every action there is an opposite and equal reaction. Newton's Third Law could be updated: For every action there is an appropriate price or cost to bear. When looking at issues such as energy, health care and agriculture, price or cost is almost always expressed in dollar terms. But other areas of the society lend themselves to a price analysis, albeit not necessarily in dollar amounts.

Take the issue of crime. Certainly, some criminologists and economists analyze the issue through a prism of dollars and cents. It costs so many thousands of dollars to feed and house prisoners. Or the suspects got away with just over $1 million dollars in small, unmarked bills. But one can also look at crime in price terms without putting a dollar figure to it. Remember, prices are signals. They tell consumers and producers what would be useful to buy and sell. Potential criminals make these same kinds of calculations.

New Pair o' Shoes

Let's take the example of Johnny Delinquent. He's a misunderstood youth who just wants what's coming to him, at least in his mind. But he's not willing to get what he wants the old-fashioned way by working and saving up enough money to get it. So he thinks about committing a crime to get what he wants. In this case, let's say a $150 pair of sneakers so he can run with his homeys.

He's been eyeing a pair in the window of a neighborhood shoe store and thinks to himself: "All I have to do is break this window, grab them and run like hell." But he also thinks: "What if the police catch me? What if there's a video surveillance camera that will catch me in the act? What kind of jail sentence will I get?" This analysis is nothing more than a price calculation. Put another way, Johnny D. is trying to determine the price of an illegal action and whether he wants to pay it, if he's caught.

To continue to the example, let's say Johnny decides that he doesn't want to pay the possible cost of jail time just for shoes. And he walks away from the window. Most of us would say he has made a wise and moral choice. But let's say he's leaning toward being unwise and immoral. He then makes some more calculations.

"Okay, let's say I'm caught," Johnny thinks to himself. "What are they going to do to me? "I'd be a first-time offender, and I'm a teenager. Hmm, my friend Hugh Ligan, got nailed last month for ripping off a PlayStation. And all he got was a suspended sentence to juvie. I saw him just yesterday." To this Johnny, the price has become clear. It's pretty low. So that low price makes him want to "buy" the activity.

Now, let's look at one more Johnny. He too is leaning toward being unwise and immoral. But his friend, Robbie Hoodlum, was caught trying to take a digital TV from a storefront window last month. Although a teenager, the court tried him as an adult, and he ended up in the state pen serving 1 to 3 years for third-degree robbery.

"Hmm," thinks Johnny. "That's pretty rough. Maybe I'll just go down to the corner and hang out." This Johnny has also analyzed the price (or cost) of an activity. He realized that it would cost a lot—his freedom being valuable to him. So he decided to avoid "buying" that activity. With this analysis, one would expect that crime rates would go down when punishment becomes more severe.

Real World Experience

But real world experience doesn't bear this out—at least at first blush. In 1984, the federal government passed the Comprehensive Crime Control Act. The act's main feature was to establish minimum sentences for various federal crimes. Congress passed the legislation in response to the perception that too many judges were letting too many criminals get off with little or no punishment. Most states followed suit. From an economic standpoint, the federal and state governments increased the price of committing crimes.

A journalist using price analysis would presume that crime rates would fall because the price of committing them had gone up. But the data don't confirm this analysis. Consider this from the FBI. From 1980 to 1984, the crime rate was dropping steadily. But in 1985, rates started picking up again.

U.S. Crime Rates

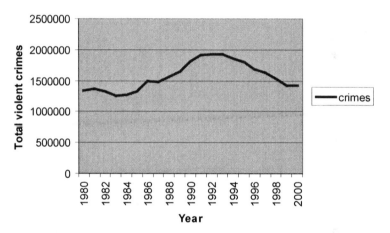

Source: U.S. Department of Justice, Bureau of Justice Statistics

Indeed, the crime rate increased until 1992 when it began to dip again. So why did the crime rates increase, even though punishments had been made more certain and severe? The answer can be found in two words—crack cocaine.

Crack cocaine spread through the cities in the mid-1980s, bringing with it an increase in a whole host of social problems Rates of homicide, burglary, assault all increased, largely attributable to the rise in the use of crack. Here is where the price-savvy journalist can again bring some analytical tools to bear. Why did crack cocaine use increase so dramatically? One only need look at crack's price and it's easy to see why more and more people started using crack.

Whereas powdered cocaine cost between $60 and $90 a gram in the mid-1980s, crack cocaine cost just a few bucks for one "rock." In addition, it provided a more intense and immediate high than powdered cocaine. So a lower price and a more desirable result led to the explosion in crack use. But the stiffer, mandatory penalties began to have their effect.

Incarceration Rates

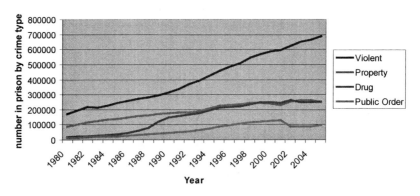

Source: U.S. Department of Justice, Bureau of Justice Statistics, Correctionsal Population in the United States, 1997, and Prisoners in 2007.

Prison populations soared starting in 1988 and 1989, and the word of the real price of committing crimes began to filter back to potential crime "consumers." Consequently, arrest rates for cocaine or heroin sales and possession peaked in 1989 and dropped thereafter.

Heroin/cocaine Arrest Rates

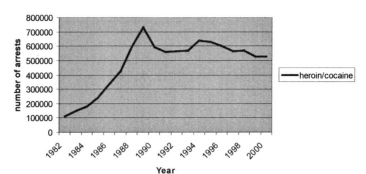

Source: U.S. Dept. of Justice, Bureau of Justice Statistics; FBI, Uniform Crime Reports.

Packin' Heat

Stiffer penalties imposed by government are one way to increase the price of crime. Another law that increases the price of crime relies, not on the police, but on the public. Some 45 states have passed laws that let members of the public carry concealed weapons. Thirty-five of those require the state to issue such permits if the applicant does not have a police record or evidence of mental illness.

As shown in research by economist John Lott and confirmed by dozens of other economists, states that allow citizens to carry concealed weapons saw drops in violent crime. One study suggested that every year the concealed carry law is in effect, murder rates decline between 1.5 and 2.3 percent.

Looking at it another way, states that don't have a concealed carry law have higher rates of violent crime, including murder, rape and aggravated assault. The media rarely report these data. Members of the media, instead, tend to play up efforts to control gun ownership.

They fail to realize that gun control laws makes the potential price of crime much lower, because an unarmed victim is unlikely to inflict any pain on the criminal. Not everybody is Chuck Norris, after all. But when a potential victim can pull a gun and shoot the assailant, the price of crime has just gone up.

Of course, there are other factors in the fluctuation in crime rates. Economic conditions, the aging of the at-risk population (most crimes are committed by young men) and family disintegration all play a part in decisions to commit crime. But one cannot overlook the effect of the price of crime in explaining different trends.

POSSIBLE EXERCISES

- *Put yourself in the role of potential criminal. Examine your decision process when considering stealing a plasma TV worth more than $1,200 and one worth about $200. You should know the laws of the state and likely punishment for that type of crime.*

- *Compare murder rates in states with and without a death penalty over the same time period.*

- *Discuss drug usage trends with regard to drug charge imprisonment rates.*

CHAPTER 9

SOCIAL ISSUES

As discussed in previous chapters, government laws often affect the price of an activity—especially where money is concerned. But laws can also affect the price of an activity where money is of little or no concern.

Take the issue of marriage. Sure, there are all sorts of tax and insurance laws that affect marriage. But what about divorce? Have government policies changed the price of divorce? A journalist sensitive to the issue of price would have to say "yes."

In the 1960s, because of the changing definitions of women's role in society, states began passing no-fault or unilateral divorce laws. These laws relaxed the standards of obtaining a divorce. A spouse didn't have to prove the other was unfaithful or dangerous. Instead, all a spouse had to cite were "irreconcilable differences," and the divorce was likely granted. Indeed, irreconcilable differences became a synonym for "I want a divorce." And they were granted.

Courting Divorce

In 1966, the divorce rate in the United States was about 2.4 per 1,000 persons. By 1981, the divorce rate more than doubled, peaking around 5.3 percent. Considered another way, the divorce rate rose by 0.2 to 0.3 divorces a year for a decade and a half.

Yet, the divorce rate began to slide downward after 1982, to around 3.6 divorces per 1,000 persons in 2007. Several answers have been offered for the drop: there are fewer marriages occurring, higher incomes help remove money pressures from a marriage and people marry later.

But another answer might be found in the pricing of a divorce. After the price of divorce became known to people—troubled children, loneliness, stress and poorer health—fewer people were willing to pay that high a price. Politicians have also noticed that high price. States have passed programs to strengthen marriage by informing people of its benefits and, by extension, the costs of ending that marriage. Washington has also passed such a program—the Health Marriage Initiative. The results of these programs have been mostly mixed, but their existence still shows an awareness of the price of divorce.

The government has played with prices on another personal issue, namely, abortion. As most journalists know, the Supreme Court ruled in *Roe v. Wade* that essentially abortions were legal. And that's the wording the media usually use to describe the landmark ruling. What few reporters do is look at the ruling from the standpoint of prices.

Prior to *Roe*, only a handful of states, California and New York among them, allowed abortions. The rest had bans of varying degrees. A few exceptions were granted to save the life of the mother or to end the product of rape or incest. For the most part, though, states did not allow legal abortions. Thus getting an abortion before *Roe* involved paying a high price – for starters, a woman usually had to disobey a law with criminal penalties.

The Price of Abortion

To avoid those penalties, women had to travel to states where abortion was legal. And not many women were willing to pay that price. In 1972, the year before *Roe*, the abortion rate was 13 abortions per 1,000 women aged 15-44 years. But after *Roe* lowered the price of abortion, more women were encouraged to "buy."

By the peak year of 1980, the rate had almost doubled to 25 per 1,000 women. In the two decades after *Roe*, the abortion rate hovered around 23 or 24 per 1,000 women.

Here again, though, the rate has declined in recent years. From 1997 to 2000, the abortion rate hovered between 16 and 20. Could it be that the price women had to pay for abortion was greater than they predicted?

According to the Elliot Institute, a nonpartisan group that specializes in studying the aftereffects of abortion found that 2 percent of women who have abortions have had "major" complications afterward.

"The nine most common 'major' complications are infection, excessive bleeding, embolism, ripping or perforation of the uterus, anesthesia complications, convulsions, hemorrhage, cervical injury, and endotoxic shock."

The effects aren't limited to the physical.

"Within 8 weeks after their abortions, 55% expressed guilt, 44% complained of nervous disorders, 36% had experienced sleep disturbances, 31% had regrets about their decision, and 11% had been prescribed psychotropic medicine by their family doctor," the Institute reported.

Other factors help explain the drop, as well. All but a handful of states have passed laws that have increased the price of abortion— parental notice and consent requirements for teenaged girls, waiting times, informed consent and reporting requirements. These added to the price of abortion, as did the growing knowledge of abortion's medical and psychological effects.

Altered States

Finally, let's turn to another social issue—drug and alcohol use. (Ahhh, that got your attention, didn't it?) Much of the reporting today regarding the legalization of drugs—particularly marijuana— centers on how it's not that different from alcohol, and how it's helpful in treating cancer and glaucoma patients.

Leaving aside the merits of the arguments for or against, let's look at the price of drinking and doing drugs. No, not the $4.99 a six-pack or $30 (CK) a bag. Rather, let's look at the price that government imposes on those two activities.

Currently, the government places a high price on drug use and a lower price on alcohol use. And the results are predictable. There's more alcohol use than illegal drug use. In 2004, some 61 percent of adults had at least one drink. That's compared to 37 percent who have tried marijuana in their lifetimes.

And when the government passed a law making the price of drinking higher—the 1930s era Prohibition—the public did less drinking. While data on alcohol consumption in that time period is not available, researchers have found that the incidence of cirrhosis of the liver and arrests for drunkenness both plummeted in 1920, the year Prohibition was enacted. Indeed, they had started dropping the year before that, as it looked more and more like Prohibition would pass. After it passed, the number of arrests and cases of cirrhosis rose gradually. But in 1933, when Prohibition was repealed, these numbers rose sharply.

U.S. Cirrhosis Death Rate 1910-2000

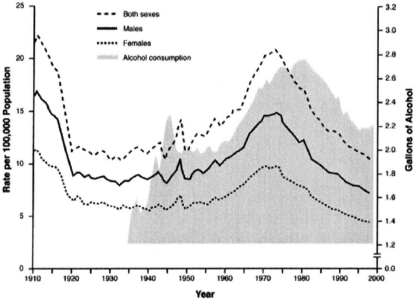

Shaded area: per capita alcohol consumption for years 1935-1999: Source: Nephew, T.M.; Williams, G.D.; Yi, H.–Y.; et al. *Surveillance Report #59: Apparent Per Capita Alcohol Consumption: National, State and Regional Trends, 1977–99*. Washington, DC: National Institute of Alcohol Abuse and Alcoholism, 2002.

Mortality rate data source: Yoon, Y.–H.; Yi, H.; Grant, B.F.; et al. *Surveillance Report #57: Liver Cirrhosis Mortality in the United States, 1970–98.* Washington, DC: National Institute on Alcohol Abuse and Alcoholism, 2001.

This analysis does not argue for or against no-fault divorce, abortion, prohibition and drug legalization. But it does show what happens when the price of an action is lowered or increased. People respond to these signals.

POSSIBLE EXERCISES

- *Total all the costs associated with divorce. Include fees, but also personal costs. Total all the benefits.*

- *What possible increases in "price" could account for the recent drop in the abortion rate?*

- *What costs do you or could you incur if you tried to buy alcohol as a minor? List them.*

CHAPTER 10

AGRICULTURE

Have you ever dropped your favorite pen behind your desk, down among the computer wires? It finds its way to the bottom of the black spaghetti, and you wonder how you ever set that mess up. Keep that image in mind.

Now think about what happens in federal agricultural policy. If anything, it's worse than the computer wire spaghetti. Through a complicated system of price controls, regulations and supply limits, the federal government interferes with prices in the agriculture marketplace.

Remember the Bicycle Manufacturers Relief Act in Chapter 4? In that example, the government sets the price of bicycles way above what the public wants to pay, but promises the manufacturers a guaranteed price? Everybody, even your mom, gets into the bicycle business to make those big profits.

Well, the federal government has been promising certain farmers that guaranteed price for more than 70 years. And the results have been predictable, for the journalist who understands prices.

Here's how it "works." The government sets a target price that is above the market price for some 12 crops. This price is what the government says would be "fair" for farmers to get. The government also gives loans to farmers each year to help them with their planting costs. The farmers have to pay the loans back, but if they can't sell their crop on the open market, farmers can use their crop to settle the loan.

To further complicate the system, the federal government makes direct payments to farmers, based on their acreage. And it makes what are called counter-cyclical payments if the market price plus the direct payment doesn't equal the target price.

Other aspects of the system involve payments for taking some land out of production for conservation purposes, as well as when disasters strike.

Direct government payments

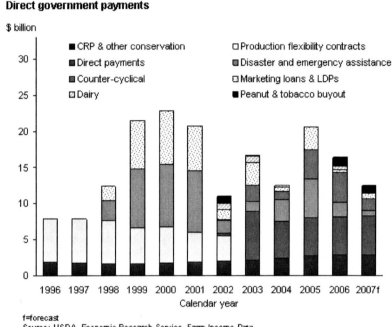

$ billion

Legend:
- ■ CRP & other conservation
- ■ Direct payments
- ■ Counter-cyclical
- □ Dairy
- □ Production flexibility contracts
- ▨ Disaster and emergency assistance
- ▨ Marketing loans & LDPs
- ■ Peanut & tobacco buyout

Calendar year

f=forecast
Source: USDA, Economic Research Service, Farm Income Data,
http://www.ers.usda.gov/Data/FarmIncome/, February 2007.

So let's see. The government guarantees a price above the market level, through loans, price supports and direct payments, and will take crops as payment for loans. What happens then?

That's right. Surpluses. The table below shows the amount of those surpluses in different crops in 2006. Some of the surpluses in feed grains and wheat goes into what is called the Food Security Commodity Reserve. Like the Strategic Petroleum Reserve, this reserve is held in the event of a national need for food. But given the incentives farmers have to grow lots of crops, a food catastrophe is hard to imagine.

U.S. Crop Surpluses 2006	
Crop	**Surplus in millions**
corn (bushels)	1,365
sorghum (bushels)	7
barley (bushels)	36
Feed grains (pounds)	9230
wheat (pounds)	18,766
cheese (pounds)	0
dried milk (pounds)	49,153
rice (hundred pounds weight)	57
soybeans (bushels)	965
sugar (pounds)	0
cotton (bales)	5
peanuts (pounds)	51,023

Source: Farm Service Agency, USDA

Direct intervention in the pricing mechanism isn't the only way the government tinkers with prices. Another way is through so-called marketing orders. These binding agreements allow growers of some 39 crops to set standards of quality, standardize packages and containers, regulate the flow of products to the market, establish reserves for certain crops and provide production and market research, and market development programs.

Let's take each in order, and see what, if any, effect they will have on price.

1) Standards of quality—These standards involve much more than just safety. They regulate size, appearance and shape. So growers in a certain region can dictate what a "good" orange is, for example, and include only those pieces of fruit that are deemed "good." All other oranges, whether they're perfectly healthy or not, can't be sold under the marketing order. These limits on supply clearly keep prices higher for the growers and for consumers.

2) Packages and cartons—If a carton of produce does not

meet the standards established by the marketing order, that produce can't be sold. That is, unless and until a "proper" carton is secured. Here again is another way to limit supply and keep prices high.

3) Flow of Product—While the other two indirectly limit supply, this gives growers power to control how much fruit or produce ever gets to market, even if it meets the standards above. Talk about incentives to keep prices high.

4) Establish Reserves—Nonperishable crops can be stored under marketing orders, thereby limiting supply again.

5) Research and Marketing—This power gives growers a lot of influence in the marketing of produce. They have more advertising dollars to spend than an individual grower does and can effectively minimize competition from smaller rivals. And what happens when competition is blocked? Higher prices.

A special mention should be made about dairy marketing orders. Here the order directly dictates at what price dairy products can be sold. Prices depend on what kind of product is being sold —ranging from butter to skim milk—on the butterfat content in the product and on the distance from Minnesota and Wisconsin. The farther from those two states, the higher the price. These prices, of course, largely come from input, you guessed it, by dairy farmers. And their incentives are to keep those prices as high as they can.

To make all these complicated laws and regulations benefit the farmer, though, requires one more government initiative—import restrictions. To state it simply, these import restrictions either impose a tariff on imported farm products to make their price equal to domestic prices, or they limit the amount of the product that can be imported.

Take sugar, for instance. The current law on sugar price supports put the price of sugar grown domestically at 18 cents a pound. The world price fluctuates between 6 cents and 10 cents a pound. But an import quota—a cap on the amount of imports—means that the price of imported sugar is close to that of domestic sugar. And the result is again predictable for the journalist who understands prices. Candy manufacturers, a main buyer of sugar, are leaving the United States and moving abroad to take advantage of the lower sugar prices.

No Sugar Tonight

Year	Quantity (in millions of lbs.)	Value (in millions of dollars)
1997	6593	13,565
1998	6546	13,569
1999	6221	13,082
2000	6258	13,503
2001	5882	13,458
2002	5810	13,355
2003	5799	13,885
2004	5766	14,627

Source: U.S. Census Bureau, Population Division, Table NA-EST2004-01

The table shows shipments by U.S. candy makers from 1997 to 2004 and the steady drop is obvious. Chicago, which once styled itself as the candy capital of the United States, now just has one candy maker still there, a half-dozen others having relocated outside the country.

To be sure, Americans pay a lot less of their household income for food. But that's because U.S. incomes are generally higher than the rest of the world. If the federal government weren't so heavily entwined in the agriculture sector, though, Americans would pay even lower prices.

POSSIBLE EXERCISES

- *Track the price of corn before and after the government increased its ethanol requirements.*

- *How many and what type of farmers typically receive support payments?*

- *How many and what type of farmers do not receive support payments?*

- *What is the most recent value of supported crops vesus unsupported crops?*

CHAPTER 11

LABOR

Want a raise?

Well, duh. Of course you do. So with that motivation, you work hard. You look for ways to improve your company's product. You look for ways for your company to become more efficient. You prove your worth to the company and the financial rewards will follow.

Members of Congress are the big exception. They vote on their own pay, and it doesn't take a 200 IQ to figure out that they've been able to justify raises for themselves and often. Every once in a while, though, members of Congress feel like spreading the wealth by requiring higher salaries for certain groups of people. They figure it's a good vote-getting strategy—increase someone's pay by law and that person is likely to vote for the one who required the increase.

But it's not white collar workers, athletes and entertainers they "help." Rather, they pass laws to benefit workers at the other end of the scale. More specifically, they vote to increase the minimum wage, all in the name of helping the working poor. And they do it a lot. From 1937, when the first minimum wage law was passed, to 2007, Congress has increased the minimum wage 18 times.

The media coverage of these efforts goes something like this Sept. 1, 2007, report from the Boston Globe:

"New Hampshire workers who earn minimum wage are getting a raise today."

"The federal government raised the minimum wage 70 cents to $5.85 an hour in July, the first increase in a decade. And today, the state minimum wage goes up to $6.50."

"State law gives workers the higher of the two rates."

"Next fall, the state rate will go up to $7.25."

Most reporters see such wage hikes as a raise in pay. They don't, or at least rarely, see what it means to the people who are required by law to pay that higher wage. And they never call the minimum wage what it is, namely a price control.

For after all, what is a wage but the price of labor? It's the amount of money an employer is willing to pay to buy your labor. You, like the storeowner in a retail market, want to get as much as you can. But you realize that, again like that storeowner, others are offering the same labor, but at lower rates. You have to lower your price to meet the competition so that it hovers just above what it would cost you to provide that labor—the cost of production.

That cost is made up of the education and experience you've had. That cost also may reflect a potential employer's prediction about your future success in the job—how many hours you would put in, how many new ideas you would have, how many customers you might bring to the business.

Labor costs therefore act just like prices in a retail market. They are subject to competitive pressures and come to rest just above the cost of producing that labor. That's why companies don't pay teenagers hundreds of thousands of dollars to become chief executive officers. Teenagers' "production" costs—as measured in their skill levels—are way below that level, so it would be a waste of the companies' money. On the other end of the scale, companies can't find CEOs for $10 an hour—their production costs are much higher.

But we've already seen what can happen when government gets in the business of setting prices. With health care and education, these government-imposed price controls are set below what it costs to produce those goods and services. Shortages develop because the producers are losing money at those mandated price levels.

With the minimum wage, the government has set a price that is above the cost of producing labor. That is, above the cost of labor by new, untrained or unskilled workers. In a market for labor that didn't have a minimum wage, these types of workers would find jobs at lower salaries. Then, after working for a while, that person's production cost goes up, because that worker has put in more time and learned more. He or she will get a raise (the good old-fashioned way).

A minimum wage is above that type of laborer's worth (or cost of production), and, as with certain agricultural goods, price controls set above the cost of production lead to surpluses. In this case, it's not a surplus of goods or services, it's a surplus of workers. There are a lot of workers willing to work for that higher wage, but fewer buyers (employers) who want to pay that higher price. Stated another way, a surplus of workers translates to higher unemployment levels.

Real world experience bears out this theory. Consider the unemployment rate of teenagers. They are unskilled, and make up the single biggest age group earning the minimum wage. The Labor Department reported in 2006 that "(a)bout half of workers earning $5.15 or less were under age 25, and about one-fourth of workers earning at or below the minimum wage were age 16-19." And those are the teenagers who actually find work. The unemployment rate for young people aged 16 to 24 in 2006 was more than 2 1/2 times the national rate (11.2 percent vs. 4.5 percent). And young black Americans had an unemployment rate almost five times the national rate (24.7 percent vs. 4.5 percent).

Here's a quick explanation—this from the Heritage Foundation, a conservative think tank in Washington, D.C.:

"Employers hire unskilled workers because they will work for less than workers who are more skilled. However, if an employer must pay $7.25 an hour to both a skilled and an unskilled job applicant, he will always hire the more productive worker. Research shows that employers change who they employ when the minimum wage rises: They hire more skilled workers and fewer unskilled and disadvantaged workers. Minority teenagers are particularly likely to lose out."

Let's take a simple example. Take you, for instance. You've just landed your first job—sales associate at a local store. You're earning the minimum wage—say $5.15 an hour. It's not great, but it lets you buy another CD or two a month.

Then you hear of talk of increasing the minimum wage. Whoo-hoo! Make that an extra three or four CDs a month. But you've noticed that, amid this talk, your boss is looking grim and worried. You realize that he's the one that's going to have to pay that wage. But surely, he can afford it, right?

So you ask him about it. And he replies with this range of options. "If they raise the minimum wage, kid, one of three things is going to happen.

"One, I may have to fire you and make do myself working the store.

"Two, you're going to have work harder and faster, because I won't be able to hire anyone else to help.

"Three, I may just have to shut down the business."

Huh? With two of those options, you don't have a job. And the third—working harder and faster—doesn't sound like too much fun, either. So you tell your boss, "It's okay. I don't need that raise. I want to keep my job and I'm willing to work for what I'm making now."

A tired smile crawls across your boss' face. "You and I won't have any choice, kid, if Congress passes that increase. I mean, I could pay a lot of money in fines and maybe even go to jail. . .But thanks, anyway."

Your boss is not just blowing smoke. In study after study, both by academics and the government, a minimum wage increase leads to an increase in unemployment among the unskilled workforce. Here's how two economists, David Neumark and William Wascher, put it after reviewing a whole range of minimum wage studies in the 1990s:

"(A)mong the papers we view as providing the most credible evidence, almost all point to negative employment effects, both for the United States as well as for many other countries."

They went on to say: "(T)he studies that focus on the least-skilled groups provide relatively overwhelming evidence of stronger disemployment effects for these groups."

Quick translation. Negative employment effects means employment rates fall and disemployment means lost jobs or never-obtained jobs.

With these kinds of effects, why does Congress (and other levels of government) continue to increase the minimum wage? The answer, as with all matters related to government, is political. A politician can seem responsive to the needs of the working poor, the little guy. And it doesn't cost a dime of taxpayer money.

There's another reason that has more to do with money than perception. And it starts with labor unions. Unions have always argued for higher minimum wages. Not because their members are making the minimum (the average union wage in 2006 was more than $21.50 an hour), but because the higher unemployment that results from a minimum wage hike means less competition for jobs that union members hold.

Here's another way to look at it: "As long as union members earn wages above the minimum rate, their positions are made more secure by the government policy that eliminates those who might undercut the union wage. People willing to work for less than the government's minimum are not allowed into the labor market at all. Indeed, union leader Edward T. Hanley stated in a catering industry employees' publication, "The purpose of the minimum wage is to . . . provide a floor from which we can upgrade your compensation through collective bargaining.'" And because unions give millions of dollars in campaign contributions every election cycle, they tend to get what they want—especially when Democrats control the legislature.

That politicians are aware of these negative effects of minimum wage hikes, there is little doubt. Rep. Ron Paul, R-Texas, asked this insightful question during the debate on the latest increase to the minimum wage: "I would ask my colleagues, if the minimum wage is the means to prosperity, why stop at $6.65—why not $50, $75, or $100 per hour?"

Indeed, why not? Because no one would pay those wages, and unemployment would shoot through the roof. But a little increase will have just a little effect, politicians reason. And those who are affected—the poor, the unskilled, the young—don't vote much anyway, now do they? So for those who keep their jobs after an increase in the minimum wage, especially union members, it's a no-brainer. But for all those who lose their jobs, or who can't get a job, a minimum wage increase has real, negative effects.

POSSIBLE EXERCISES

- *Track the teenage unemployment trends after each increase in the minimum wage.*

- *Track the payroll growth numbers after each increase in the minimum wage.*

- *Do a story on how a small business handles wage increases—required or not.*

CHAPTER 12

MONOPOLIES

You've already admitted that you'd like to be able to raise your salary. What if you owned a business where you could set prices almost wherever you wanted? Yep, there's no other competition. You've cornered the market. Congratulations. You now enjoy the benefits of a monopoly. And the money should start rolling in.

But wait. Who's that upstart company who's making and selling the product you make? Arrgh. There goes your monopoly. You're going to have to lower prices in order to compete with the upstart. And he'll lower prices and so on, until the price nears the cost of production.

But what if the government passes a law that prevents upstart competitors? You'd be all for it, right? You're dang skippy, you would.

Well, you might want to try the cable TV business. Because that's exactly what thousands of local governments have done—passed a law that prevents competition. This, despite a range of federal laws that ban monopolies. The Sherman Antitrust Act is the first of these, and it's been amended since by the Clayton Act, and other laws in 1936, 1950, 1964 and 1976.

These laws ban such practices as so-called predatory pricing, where companies charge prices lower than the cost of production, figuring that any competitors couldn't absorb these losses.

Another banned practice is extracting low prices from suppliers because of your size or importance to the economy. But most cable companies don't have to worry about competition because of the protection they enjoy from government.

So how do cable companies get around all the federal laws banning monopolies? They do so by claiming that they do have competition—when cities award the contract for providing cable coverage. A number of cable providers make bids to the city, and the city awards the contract to the most attractive bid. But attractive doesn't necessarily mean low-priced.

Why? Because this competition does not benefit consumers, it benefits cities. Really benefits cities, with all sorts of goodies. Here's how Clint Bolick, an attorney who specializes in constitutional and regulatory issues, saw it in a policy paper from the Cato Institute, a think tank that promotes limited government.

The Denver franchise, awarded in 1982, provides an example of this process. . . Among other requirements, the franchisee must:

* pay 5 percent of its annual gross revenues as a franchise fee, plus an additional 2 percent for community programming;

* defray the city's expenses for the RFP [Requests for Proposal] process ($80,000);

* provide a $1 million construction bond and a $100,000 letter of credit;

* grant $1.5 million in loans and capital to small businesses and minority groups;

* wire the entire city according to a fixed construction schedule based on political rather than practical considerations;

* agree to pay $1,000 penalty per day for franchise violations;

* submit to rate regulation;

* allow the city to veto programming changes;

* set aside all or part of 22 channels for programming access, and cede editorial control over them!; and

* build studios and other facilities for access to selected special-interest groups at a cost of $7.34 million; and provide an emergency override system that enables city officials to turn on subscribers' sets, adjust the volume, and broadcast "emergency" messages into their homes at any hour of the day or night.

In exchange, the franchisee receives a de facto exclusive 15-year franchise and is insulated from some of the effects of competition through a guaranteed rate of return.

Cities argue that cable TV is a natural monopoly. They say more than one provider would unnecessarily disrupt the smooth flow of commerce and transportation in a city—ripping up streets, laying wire and securing rights-of-way.

But is it?

To hear cities and cable companies talk, you'd think a single franchise arrangement is the only thing that stands between the populace and eternal damnation. But to hear consumers in places like Troy and Montgomery, Alabama, competition is not only nice but a cause for action if it's ever taken away. That's right. These two cities have two cable providers competing for customers. This competition keeps prices down and it keeps service up.

Consider the rates for basic service offered by Troy Cable in Troy—$33. Charter Communications, which also serves Troy, charges $29. In addition, Troy Cable and Charter will also schedule specific appointments with customers to meet them at their house. That instead of the "sometime in the afternoon, I'll get there when I get there" attitude that monopoly providers usually have.

A similar tale can be told about prices and service in Montgomery, where two companies compete for customers. But as of late 2007, these two cities were among just a handful of municipalities that have required competition.

That may be changing. In the early 2000s, the federal government considered rules to void all the single-franchise agreements In addition, a number of states are passing laws that ban local government franchises. But these states replace local franchise agreements with a state agreement. Supporters say this will open up competition at the local level, as all cable companies pay a fee to the state and they are allowed to operate in the state.

But what's to prevent state regulators from unofficially granting a monopoly to a provider, say, in exchange for a few goodies (can you say more goodies?). Not much. Indeed, as long as the permission to operate is controlled by politicians, monopolies will continue to be set up—the incentives are too great.

Companies get to price their service at high levels, while the politicians get a range of benefits, from campaign donations to pork barrel spending to cash from bribes. And consumers get what they get and have to like it.

What about other so-called natural monopolies, such as water, sewage, gas and electricity services? Or public transportation? Consider the history of electricity. After Thomas Edison built the first generating plant in the 1870s, a number of companies sprang up to sell the service.

First, the electric companies went after businesses—and wealthy people. Soon, though, the companies saw possible buyers everywhere.

By 1920, the major cities all had electricity, with companies competing for customers, each with its own wires and poles. But politicians, looking for voters, began passing franchise monopolies on the condition that all houses were served, even in sparse rural areas, which are more expensive to wire. In exchange for the monopoly, the electric company agreed to have its rates regulated by —you guessed it—a government agency.

The agency is supposed to keep prices to consumers reasonable. But most electric companies also argue that they should have a guaranteed rate of return—supposedly to keep maintenance up and innovations coming.

But what are "reasonable" rates? Does some brainy electrical engineer accountant sit in a basement and come up with a price? Hardly. The price is set up the governing body of the regulatory agency. And since these people are politicians, they set prices at a level that benefits them. Prices can't be too high, or consumers would complain.

But they also try to keep the electric companies happy with higher rates. The unspoken power that the electric companies have is that they could turn off the power and hold up consumers for outrageous rates.

The potential abuses of monopoly power have allegedly been recognized in a number of states. They have restructured their electricity policies, claiming that this "deregulation" will help local ratepayers. Unfortunately, while some states say they have competition after restructuring, the government is still heavily involved.

Virginia, for instance, said it would allow consumers to choose from different electric providers. But it capped rates for five years. Sound like a price control? Yep, it sure does. And when energy costs soared, power companies were losing money even faster. But demand at the lower rates remained at the same rate. So when the price caps came off, rates shot up in order to meet the losses the companies had incurred.

A similar tale can be told in all the states that supposedly freed up the electricity market. Ironically, supporters of this deregulation said that the deregulation and competition would mean lower prices for consumers. But none of the states allowed full competition to work, regulating much of the marketplace. And that meant higher prices. These price spikes, naturally, prompted calls for restoring the old system. But prices there are dependent on government price controls, not on competition.

Public transportation is another sector, like electricity, that went from competition to monopoly status. In the 1960s, there were bus and subway companies that competed for riders. But a quarter of them were not making any money— they were going out of business. Those inefficient companies couldn't compete. Enter the politicians. They saw more votes, as well as campaign support, if they began to subsidize mass transit.

So in the early 1960s, Congress passed laws that gave $40 million to public transit companies, which had consolidated into monopolies. Today, that figure tops $4 billion. But ridership has plummeted, prices have soared and service is mostly subpar—missed schedules, dirty buses and subway cars, and less crime prevention. The monopolies, combined with federal money, means that transit companies have little incentive to hold down costs or improve service. But when monopolies are broken up and competition installed, prices drop and consumers benefit.

Another case in point is long-distance telephone service. In the early days of phone service, again there were a number of providers. But government stepped in and set up a monopoly in phone service, Ma Bell (aka AT&T) in 1913. Again, politicians wanted voters, so it forced AT&T to serve more expensive rural consumers. In exchange, AT&T got a monopoly. In order to meet the government's mandate that it serve home consumers, AT&T charged high rates for long-distance rates and kept residential rates lower.

And so it remained a monopoly until 1984, when, as a result of a Justice Department lawsuit, AT&T agreed to break itself up. Pushing for this so-called divestiture was the MCI phone company and big businesses, tired of subsidizing home rates.

So the Justice Department ordered Ma Bell to sell off its local phone services to seven regional companies, known as Baby Bells. Competition entered the long-distance market and predictably, prices fell. Indeed, from 1984 to 2002, prices after adjusting for inflation fell by about 90 percent.

Real Interstate Long Distance Rates and AT&T Market Share of Long Distance Revenues

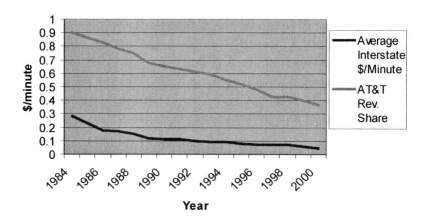

Sources: Robert Crandall, Brookings Institution, U.S. Justice Department

But prices to residential consumers rose. Yet there has been little deregulation of local phone service. So prices remain high, and determined by government.

For instance, the Federal Communications Commission reports that household expenditures on all phone use (including long-distance service) rose 128 percent from 1984, the year of AT&T's break-up, to 2004. For comparison, inflation only went up 82 percent over the same time period.

To be sure, part of that increase was a result of more spending on cell phones. But said another way, telephone spending went up half-again as much as inflation from 1984 to 2004.

Check out another result of government-set prices. From 1995 to 2005, household spending on local service went up 20 percent. But spending on long-distance service went down 62 percent. Part of the reason for the increase is the government's continued setting of rates. But adding to the mix is a little present the federal government gave telephone consumers. Known as a subscriber line charge, as of 2007 it was almost $6 a line. Two lines, nearly $12. This charge represents a payment consumers make for gaining access to long-distance phone lines.

To be sure, local phone companies are facing some competition from cell phones, and some observers see a day when landlines are obsolete. And while there is some regulation of the cell phone airwaves, prices are set by competition for the most part. (Judging from the quantity of cell phone commercials in prime time every night, there...is...a...lot...of...competition.)

Some in the media take some pleasure in pointing out that free markets in these so-called natural monopolies just don't work. "Competition was supposed to lower prices in deregulated states. But faster-rising rates there are spurring a backlash," blared the Christian Science Monitor in an April 2006 article. To its credit, the Monitor quoted liberally from people who understand prices.

John Anderson, president of the Electricity Consumers Resource Council, said: "We were deregulation's first supporters. But all we've really done is go from one regulatory structure to a new one that is less customer friendly."

The New York Times is no friend of competition, nor do its reporters know much about it. Consider the unstated premise behind these words from a November 2007 article in the Gray Lady of News:

"In New England and the the Middle Atlantic states, as well

in as Britain, Chile and Argentina, all places that have restructured electricity markets, regulators have had to adjust market rules to correct flaws."

The flaws seem to exist in the market, not in the restructuring, according to this reporter. But competition will always produce lower prices, if government leaves the market pretty much alone. It is only when governments get involved in setting market rules (other than the sanctity of contracts) that competition fails to work. And it is in these so-called natural monopolies that government has set up the most rules, leaving competition waiting for a bus.

POSSIBLE EXERCISES

- *Design a way to allow competition in the local telephone marketplace.*

- *Compare the market in any of today's "monopolies" to the markets in railroads and air travel in the 1970s.*

- *Discuss the effects of regulated markets and unregulated markets on innovation.*

CHAPTER 13

FINANCIAL MARKETS

As recently as 25 years ago, when the subject of the stock market came up, most people thought of some old, fat guy in striped pants, smoking a cigar, and buying and selling stocks. The quintessential fat cat. And there was some truth behind this stereotype. Only 5 percent of U.S. households had investments in the stock market.

In 2007, however, that number has topped 50 percent. So investment is not a foreign word to Americans any more. And more and more people are learning to read financial statements, more and more are watching the business networks or business shows on TV, and more and more are watching government policies to see if those will affect specific investments.

And, of course, the chief way to keep track of investments is their price. In these markets, investors make decisions every day based in large part on the price of the investment and whether they think that price will increase. If it does, the value of their investment increases. It is pretty obvious why investors buy these products—they're looking for a profit on their investment.

But why does the stock market exist? Why do companies offer stocks? One word sums it up: Growth. Companies want to expand their business. They want to reach new markets. They want to spend more on research and development to come up with the next big thing. They want to hire more people to increase output. And all of these actions require funds.

So when a company needs to raise money, it often sells shares in the company. A stock is nothing more than part of a company. So if a company issues 100 million shares, and you have one share, you own 1/100 millionth of the company. But keep in mind that even though a company may issue 100 million shares, it doesn't sell all of them to the public. Indeed, it will keep a significant number under company control. This nest egg of stocks then provides the company with funds to back any loans it may want to take out. And it may want to take out loans, again, to grow. Therefore the company has an incentive to increase the value of each share of stock. It gives them access to more funds to borrow.

And how does a company increase the value of a stock? Essentially a company boosts the value of its stock by taking actions that impress investors in the market. Those actions all are geared to increasing the company's profits. The actions range from discovering new products, services and consumers, or cutting back on expenses. Investors, seeing a company taking these actions, try to buy shares of that company.

You might ask: Why spend that money? It's an expense to the investors, right? Sure it is. But investors aren't looking at today. They're looking anywhere from six to 12 months in the future. They believe that the company is going to continue to be attractive to investors, and want to have stocks they can sell when those new investors come looking for a stock. The increased desire to buy that stock will lead investors into a bidding war.

Let's take a simple example. Investor X has bought shares in WhizBang Gizmos. He bought 100 shares at $5 a share. He thinks WhizBang is going places. He likes the research WhizBang is doing and figures that the gizmo maker will make bigger profits.

Sure enough, WhizBang introduces a new and improved gizmo that has consumers clamoring for it. The profit picture looks great ahead. Investors Y and Z see the new gizmo and think that WhizBang will do even better. So they seek to buy shares. But Investor X doesn't want to sell, unless he can make some real money. So he lets Y and Z make some offers. They each have calculated how much they think the price of shares of WhizBang will rise to. Y believes they will top out at $10, but Z is convinced that these share prices will reach $20.

So the bidding begins. Y says she'll pay $6 a share. If that share reaches $10, as she predicts, and she sells her WhizBang shares, she'll realize a profit of some 67 percent.

But Investor Z thinks the price will go even higher, so he bids $7 a share. He figures he will make nearly a 200 percent gain. Y wants those shares, and she's willing to pony up. So she bids $8 a share, figuring that a 20 percent profit is still pretty good.

Z comes back with a bid of $10. If his calculations are correct, he stands to get a 100 percent profit. Y doesn't like that calculation so she stops bidding, and Z is happy to snap up the shares at $10.

This demand for WhizBang shares creates a competition. And like the demand between consumers for goods at the lowest possible price, investors compete for shares that will provide them the highest profits. The difference is that investors try to predict the future, whereas consumers are more interested in what kind of deal they can get now.

If you look at a different scenario, share prices fall. For instance, if a company fails to make a profit or if its new product doesn't sell as well as expected, investors will sell their shares so as not to lose too much money on their investments.

So in the stock market, predictions of the future help determine prices. If the future is rosy, buy. If it's glum, sell.

So what goes into those predictions? Of course, a lot of it depends on what a company produces. Investors looking at a silicon chip company probably don't care that much about drought affecting the cranberry crop. But there are factors that affect all investments.

One, obviously, is the state of the economy. If the economy slows or even heads downward, profits are harder to come by and investors don't put a lot of money into stocks. And because investors are looking ahead, a broad-based sell-off of stocks with prices headed lower suggest that tough economic times are on the way. Conversely, if stock prices start to rise in a faltering economy, it means investors see economic growth in six to nine months.

Finally, another factor that affects prices is government action. It's most obvious when government changes its tax policy. As discussed earlier, the government taxes profits on investments. These profits, known as capital gains, are the target of many politicians. Politicians invoke the old image of fat cats getting rich without having to work for it. So these politicians try to reap some of those profits in the form of taxes on capital gains. But, recall that all taxes do is raise the price of a good or service, so the higher the tax, the less buying there will be.

A quick review of the recent history on capital gains taxes bears out this common-sense observation.

Long-Term Capital Gains and Taxes Paid on Long-Term Capital Gains 1979-2006

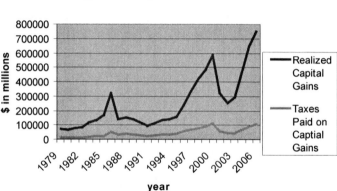

Tax Rate on Long-Term Capital Gains 1979-2006

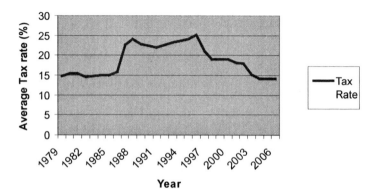

Sources: Congressional Budget Office; Department of Commerce, Bureau of
Economic Analysis; Department of the Treasury.

The data also show that when taxes on capital gains drop,
realizations—fancy word for selling shares—go up sharply. Similarly, if investors know that the rate will go up, they will sell their
shares, or realize their gains.

That's what happened in 1986. Congress passed a tax bill
that scheduled an increase in the capital gains tax rate, effective Jan.
1, 1987. Not being dummies, investors sold many of their shares so
they wouldn't have to pay the higher taxes.

The record of capital gains taxes has convinced even the
most populist lawmakers that a lower capital gains rate is beneficial.
But that still doesn't stop other politicians from looking to the stock
market for tax revenues. A handful of lawmakers over the years
have proposed a tax on every stock transaction. And we know that
whenever you tax an activity, you get less of it, all because the price
of that activity goes up.

Another factor that affects stock prices is inflation (See appendix I). One effect of inflation, at least at the beginning of an inflationary stage, is investors who had bought at lower prices earlier
want to take some profits. But, as the purchasing power of dollars
goes down, it takes more dollars to buy stocks. That higher price
level discourages investors—remember, buyers don't like high prices. So those investors who sold shares may not put their profits back
into the market. Lower stock prices mean companies' nest eggs
aren't worth as much, and they are less likely to expand.

Interestingly, stock investors don't mind a little inflation in
the economy. Stock prices rise, and investments are worth making.
But, too much inflation, and investment slows down. This is what
economists call "stagflation"—stagnant investment coupled with inflation.

Inflation, even a small amount, has even more effect on another huge investment market: bonds. While many commentators
lump stocks and bonds together, they are different investment tools.
Where stocks are shares of ownership, bonds are loans to compa-

nies. Investors still look at a company's future--is it doing well, will it continue to show profits—before they lend the companies money.

Here's the way it works: A company wants money to expand. So it offers bonds to investors at an interest rate that it agrees to pay when the bond matures. And everyone is happy as long as that interest rate is greater than the inflation rate. It's a fixed amount that the company agrees to pay. And investors figure that they will profit when inflation rates are low.

A quick example: A company offers bonds that will mature in five years and pay 6 percent of the value of the loan each year. If investors see inflation remaining where it's been historically—between 2 and 3 percent a year—they foresee a gain of 3 to 4 percent a year. If they lend $1 million, investors will gain $30,000 to $40,000 the first year, with slightly less per year for the remainder of the loan period. But if investors see inflation at 5 to 6 percent a year, there is little reason to lend money and get little or no gain from it.

Let's say, though, that a company really wants money to expand. And it can't get investors at a 6 percent interest rate. So it is forced to offer a higher interest rate. The interest rate thus becomes the price upon which buyers and sellers react. But there is one difference. In the case of bonds, competition leads to higher interest rates, as well as lower.

Here's how that works. Remember how investors look ahead? If they see a company is solid and going to be around at the end of the life of the bond, then they are willing to take a low interest rate. Why? Because the investment is virtually guaranteed. But an investors that see a company that has the chance to lose lots of money, even go out of business, want as high an interest rate as possible. Put in a phrase, the riskier the investment, the higher the interest rate.

Such risky investments can pay off big. MCI, Viacom and Turner Broadcasting all were financed with high-interest rate bonds. These bonds—known by critics as "junk bonds"—were available to companies that wanted to expand but didn't meet banks' lending criteria. Those are the investors who are willing to take risks.

Millions more investors, however, want a safer, more assured payoff. So they look for established companies for bond investments. They also can look to different levels of government, which issue bonds. States, cities, counties and public universities all can issue bonds. And municipalities have the advantage of being able to increase their cash holdings by either raising taxes or cutting programs.

That is not to say, however, that all municipal bonds are equal. Some are riskier than others, just as with corporate bonds. In the 1990s, California had spent a lot more money than it had coming in. Politicians did not want to raise taxes, as the Golden State had some of the highest income taxes among states. But the state had to make payments for programs passed by the legislature, so it went into the bond market. Investors didn't like what they saw. They refused to buy California bonds at lower rates, insisting on higher rates, because of the risk that California might go into default and be unable to pay the bonds back fully.

So California was forced to issue bonds that achieved "junk bond" levels. And this compounds its budget problems, because it will have to pay those higher interest rates. That's how competition pushes bond interest rates higher.

Competition can also push bond interest rates—the price of bonds—lower. Here's how. Let's say a good company decides to issue bonds in order to expand. Bond investors are eager to invest in such a good company. So they offer to accept a lower interest rate, which the good company is glad to get.

Why, then, are there interest rates at all? Doesn't competition drive rates down to zero? No, because of the effects of inflation. So interest rates do not go below the expected rate of inflation, otherwise investors actually lose money. And just like the auto dealer, the investor is not doing this to lose money.

There are all sorts of other types of investments—commodities, stock options, land, hedge funds, futures, etc. One other type of investment that bears special mention is a mutual fund. This is a pool of money, managed by an investment firm, that goes to buy a number of different investment options. There are stock mutual funds (the most common), bond funds, commodity funds, real estate funds. Essentially, anything you can invest in can be part of a mutual fund.

There are mutual funds that focus on stocks in transportation, high-tech, pharmaceutical and big companies, to name but a few. There are mutual funds that focus on municipal bonds, low-risk corporate bonds, and high-risk bonds. There are commodity, real estate and futures mutual funds.

But why invest in a mutual fund? Aren't you just exposing yourself to the risk of each company? No, because fund managers, are always buying and selling investment. So if a stock looks shaky, the fund manager will dump it and buy another stock with better prospects. Therefore, mutual funds reduce risk by diversifying holdings, meaning investments rarely go bad.

Indeed, if you were to have bought a mutual fund based on the Standard & Poor's 500 index, which reflects the broad market, in January 1920, you would have seen an average annual rate of growth of 7.7 percent—and that's after the effects of inflation are factored out! That period includes the Great Depression and 15 recessions since 1920.

But whatever type of investment you consider, remember: They all operate on the same principles. Investors look ahead, usually for signs of growth. They must also deal with the effects of competition, and they must accurately gauge risk. There is also a market for pessimists who are betting that an investment will drop. But these so-called short sellers also have to account for risk and competition, as well as predict the future, as well. So investment markets are reacting to price signals, albeit in slightly different ways.

And you don't have to be a fat cat to start investing.

POSSIBLE EXERCISES

- *What stocks does the Dow Jones Industrial Average represent? The S&P500?*

- *Find out who monitors the riskiness of bonds.*

- *Is there a bond rating system? If so, how does it work?*

- *Describe the process of short-selling.*

The Power of Compounding

Let's consider an example of two persons—Tom and John—who decided to secure their retirement years by two different approaches. They both start with $30,000 for investments. Tom decided to invest them in a savings account, whereas John invested them in a mutual fund.

Tom had an income that allowed him to put another $30,000 into his savings account every year. John was not in a position to do so and so far it looked like Tom had the greater premise for secure retirement years.

We will make some assumptions for this example:

- 3% inflation rate;

- Tom's account makes the exact amount necessary for the coverage of inflation;

- John's account makes 12% above inflation.

The following table represents the amounts of money that Tom and John have after a particular period of time based on the assumptions made above.

	Tom	John
After 5 years	$150,000	$47,206
After 10 years	$300,000	$83,192
After 15 years	$450,000	$146,612
After 20 years	$600,000	$258,381
After 25 years	$750,000	$455,356
After 30 years	$900,000	$802,493
After 35 years	$1,050,000	$1,414,267
After 40 years	$1,200,000	$2,492,422

Who is getting less now?

Forty years after their initial investments, the sum in John's mutual fund has grown to the outstanding $2,492,422 compared to the twice less $1,200,000 in Tom's savings account. What is the moral of the story? The lesson you should learn is that although Tom continuously invested his hard earned money in his account, he could still not get the same result as John. And that's because of compounding.

CHAPTER 14

GOVERNMENT ACTION

"I'm from the government and I'm here to help you."

This famous punch line brings a smile to most lips because most everyone has had a distasteful experience with the government. From getting your car registration to waiting for a tax refund to applying for some sort of assistance, government rarely seems to "help you" very well.

That's just at the personal level. But as the previous chapters have indicated, the government doesn't have a good track record on the big things either. Lawmakers tinker with prices, stifle supply and competition, and generally manipulate markets—usually to the detriment of everyday consumers.

You may ask: This econ stuff isn't so tough, why don't they know better? Why do they do those things when it hurts the very people who might vote for them? After all, isn't it a government of, by and for the people? Aren't lawmakers supposed to have our best interests at heart?

The answer can be found in some basic economic analysis. Much of this analysis has been conducted by a so-called public choice school of economics.* This school examines the actions of government figures and attempts to find out what motivates them to make the decisions they do. And what scholars in this field have determined is that lawmakers make very rational decisions, given their circumstances. And if those decisions aren't necessarily the

---

* A leading proponent of this school is James Buchanan of George Mason University. He won the Nobel Prize for Economics in 1986 for his work on public choice theory.

best for the people they represent, then that's where their powers of persuasion and politicking come in real handy.

Here's a brief discussion of the public choice view of things. First, unlike other economists and many in the public, public choice proponents don't start with the premise that the government can only do beneficial things. They realize that government officials and lawmakers often back policies that have a negative impact. No, make it simpler. They sometimes do things that are bad. So with that premise, public choicers ask why they do bad things. And these economists analyze officials' actions through the prism of prices and pricing.

In order to get elected, wannabe lawmakers must pay a high price. The money costs are bad enough. The average campaign for a seat in the House of Representatives in 2006 had to raise almost $1.2 million on average, a Senate candidate had to raise an average of more than $8 million. But candidates also face brutal 12- to 16-hour days, innumerable meetings with folks who have money and a severe loss of family time.

Cost of Winning an Election--House Winners 1998-2006

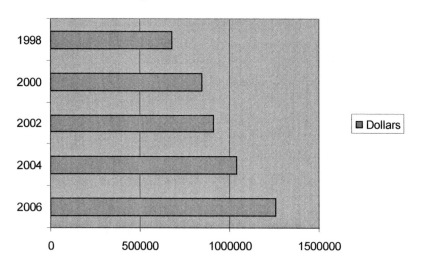

Source: Analysis of Federal Election Commission data, Brookings Institution Press, 2008

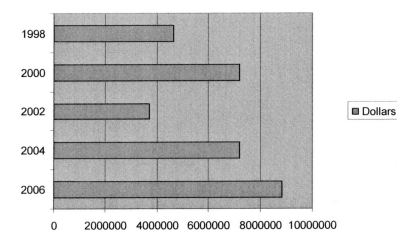

Cost of Winning an Election–Senate Winners 1998-2006

Source: Analysis of Federal Election Commission data, Brookings Institution Press, 2008

Despite this high price, there are always people willing to pay it because they believe what they might get—a seat in Congress —is worth it. That belief may be grounded for some in a desire to do good. But in others, that belief is often grounded in a desire to do well. After all, the base salary for rank-and-file members of the House and Senate is $165,000. Health insurance and retirement benefits are more generous than those found in the private sector.

And, oh the perks. There's a housing allowance, money for a staff and free mailing privileges, not to mention a members-only gymnasium, cut-rate hair cutters and a stationery store where gifts can be bought at cost. Members of the leadership get even more in salary, plus drivers and a car.

In exchange for all this, members of Congress have to analyze issues, vote and keep in touch with constituents. Plus, you get to influence the spending of trillions and trillions of dollars. As the saying goes, not bad work, if you can get it. And once candidates get that work, they want to keep it.

To do that, though, requires more money for re-election campaigns. Incumbents still have to face the voters in the next election, and, thus, they must seen to the average voter as "doing a good job." That message is usually conveyed in free newsletters and in televised campaign ads.

But newsletters and especially campaign ads rarely get into the specifics of legislation and issues. Rather, they feature warm, fuzzy images with bumper sticker sayings, such as "Elect someone who will be tough on crime" or "I'm for programs that help the middle-class."

And guess what? Voters don't really care. They know that their single vote won't likely mean much, so they have little reason to study up on the issues. So lawmakers have little reason to make votes based purely on the "public interest." Indeed, acting in the public interest may hurt his or her chances to get re-elected.

In addition, they make decisions using other people's money, not their own. So, unlike the consumer in the private sector, lawmakers have little reason to conserve spending. It's not their money, after all. This lack of incentives to act in the public interest, combined with the self-interest that lawmakers have, lead to policies that boost prices and mess up the normal functioning of a competitive marketplace.

But wait a minute, you say. Why is it in lawmakers' self-interest to pass bad laws? Let's go back to their motivation to stay in office. It takes money to do so, and who has the biggest chunks of money? It's not Joe Six-Pack. It's big groups. Businesses, unions and professions all have lots of cash because they have lots of members who pay dues. Those dues are handed out in the form of campaign donations, which lawmakers seek desperately. But those dues don't come without strings attached.

These interest groups want certain benefits from government. Those benefits range from outright subsidies to rules that limit competition. Economists call this rent-seeking. And the lawmaker, eager for cash, agrees to look out for the interests of a group. If a group spreads enough money around, a majority of lawmakers will join to help advance the group's interest.

Some examples:

—Unions want higher minimum wage rates because union

wages are largely a matter of adding a certain amount to whatever the minimum wage rate is. Also, a higher minimum wage means more unemployment—and more importantly, less competition for jobs for union workers.

—Farmers like subsidies and price supports because it guarantees them income.

—Cable systems don't like competition, so they lobby for exclusive franchise rights in different markets.

—Bigger businesses don't mind regulations because they can afford to comply with them, whereas smaller competitors are hard-pressed to meet the rule's requirements. This helps stifle the competition for bigger businesses. The same logic applies to taxes.

—In the health care field, while providers may complain about the price controls in different federal programs, they don't necessarily want to operate in a competitive environment. They'd have to provide better service at or near the price as the next provider.

—Also in health care, consumers don't mind the price controls because it means most of them pay little to nothing for health care. They'd hate to have to start spending their own money when they went to the doctor or stayed in a hospital. Lawmakers realize that voters would be ticked off if they took away their "free" health care, so they have little reason to make economically-sound reforms.

Analysts have offered different ideas on how to make lawmakers more attuned to the public interest and make better economic decisions. One school would impose a limit on the amount of time lawmakers could serve in office. In that way, members of Congress wouldn't have to worry so much about raising money for the next election.

Another school would impose a constitutional requirement to balance the federal budget. Their thinking goes that this requirement would force lawmakers to be more responsible when it comes to spending taxpayer dollars.

Others would eliminate all the perks that lawmakers get. In other words, make the job less attractive. Still others would further restrict the ability of interest groups to lobby Congress.

All of these ideas have some appeal. But few would work as intended, because lawmakers would still have control over trillions and trillions of dollars, which is power no matter how you slice. For any solution to work, it must take a lawmaker's self-interest into account. Reducing the amount of money the government spends would reduce the power of lawmakers.

Offering a big payout to lawmakers who retire after a short stint in office could also make not working in Congress attractive. The payout could go down the longer someone's in office. But since all of these would require the endorsement of members of Congress, their passage is very unlikely.

One solution that has worked in certain instances and could work on a larger scale requires no action by Congress. That solution? Better reporting, especially of economic matters. Take the health care proposal that then-First Lady Hillary Clinton was developing in 1994. Reporting helped expose some of the potential economic problems in the package. (Full disclosure: I did some of that reporting.) In the end, it died even before it reached Congress. In 2005, extensive coverage of funding a bridge to a small, barely inhabited island in Alaska led ultimately to the demise of the project two years later.

In 1993, then-Rep. Newt Gingrich, R-Ga., came up with a national strategy that helped sweep Republicans into control of the House for the first time in four decades. The GOP also took control of the Senate. That strategy? The famous (or infamous, depending on your point of view) "Contract with America."

The media covered this plan widely, often editorializing against it, and largely remaining skeptical of the 10-point plan. But they reported on it, and citizens apparently liked what they heard. Included in the contract were calls for a balanced budget amendment, stronger laws against crime, welfare reform and personal retirement accounts that enjoyed tax breaks.

Interestingly, the contract was overall an economically sound package. But only four of its provisions became law. While the House of Representatives passed every item, those that were defeated met their end either in the Senate or at the Clinton White House. Nonetheless, the coverage of the contract reached a lot of voters, who voted Republicans into power.

If reporters routinely covered all the actions of Congress with an understanding of economics, voters would be much better informed when they went to the polls. And this greater awareness would make lawmakers more likely to make economically sound decisions. Why? Because the price of making a bad vote would be removal from office, and there goes that nice work if you can get it.

Indeed, if the media would report on government with a slightly different punch line in mind, then fewer economic distortions would find their way into everyday life. That new punch line? "I'm from the government and I'm here to help...me."

POSSIBLE EXERCISES

- *One aspect of federal budgeting is that there is an automatic increase in spending built into the process. How does this fit in with public choice theory?*

- *In the House of Representatives, re-election rates regularly top 90 percent. How does this fit in with public choice theory?*

- *Find an example of your representative or senator making a vote that differs with his or her philosophy and explain why.*

INFLATION

Perhaps no other factor affects prices more than inflation. And journalists, other than knowing that prices and inflation are related, don't really understand how it happens.

One common fallacy that's reflected in the reporting on inflation is that somehow higher prices cause inflation. Here's how an Associated Press in July 2007 reported the latest government figures on inflation:

- "The Labor Department says consumer prices rose two-tenths of one percent last month.
- "It is the smallest increase in five months, despite surging food costs.
- "The modest increase was enabled by a pullback in energy prices.
- "The core Consumer Price Index, which excludes food and energy, also edged up two-tenths."

Somehow, lower energy prices seemed to hold inflation in check, while food prices helped boost it. At least according to the AP. But in reality, it's the exact opposite. Inflation causes high prices. And the cause of inflation? Government action.

Nobel Prize-winning economist Milton Friedman once wrote that "inflation is always and everywhere a monetary phenomenon." What that means is that the policies that govern a nation's money are key to understanding inflation. In short, government creates money. How much it creates and how fast determines how much inflation is in the economy.

A bumper sticker definition of inflation still sums it up nicely:

"Inflation is the result of too much money chasing too few goods."

Let's try a simple example. Let's say you and nine friends decided to start a company. You each put in $1,000 and you each own 1/10th of the company. To symbolize that ownership, you have certificates printed up that are each worth a tenth of the company. Your company sells the latest design in widgets, and your first year, you sell 1 million new and improved widgets.

Based on the first year's results, you, as a group, decide that the company is going to double its sales in the next year. So you order 10 more certificates based on the belief that they will be worth the same amount of the first 10—namely $1,000.

But sales don't grow as much as you had predicted. In fact, they don't grow at all. So now, you have two certificates that represent $1,000. In other words, the certificates are worth half what they were in the company's first year.

Now, think of money as nothing more than your share of the economy. And the government is in charge of printing those "certificates." If the economy doesn't grow as quickly as the government projects, your claims of ownership of the economy—your certificates—aren't worth as much as they were the year before. So it takes more certificates to buy the same stuff you used to buy. Expressed another way, the price of stuff has gone up because of your lower-valued certificates.

With billions and billions of transactions by millions and millions of people occurring every day, it's impossible to predict how much the economy is going to grow. And that is the basis for the government's actions on creating money.

Still, the government—in the form of the Federal Reserve—must try to create enough money to allow growth, but not so much that inflation erodes the value of that money.

Not only does the Fed affect prices with its monetary policies, it also relies on the pricing mechanism to control the money supply. Put simply, the Fed uses interest rates on loans by member Fed banks make to each other on an "overnight," or very short-term, basis. Borrowing banks may think the interest rates are too high and so won't borrow money. Conversely, banks may think that the interest rates the Fed sets are low and thus borrow money.

Less money borrowed means you don't have the so-called inflationary pressures. The opposite is true—more borrowing may increase inflationary pressures.

Keep in mind that not enough money in the economy is a problem, as well. Indeed, the Federal Reserve interest rates peaked in 1929-30 but fell by some 30 percent over the next eight years. With no money for growth, it's no wonder the Depression was so Great.

In today's world, the Fed doesn't want to repeat that mistake, but even minor moves either way in the money supply can spur growth or impede it. Fed watchers, therefore, pay close attention to the central bank's actions, and make investments based on their projections of the economy.

In simple terms, if the money supply goes up (when interest rates fall), investors look to stocks because companies have more money to invest in expansion and therefore growth. But if the money supply falls (when interest rates rise), investors turn to the bond market because the repayment rate stays the same.

A simple example can help illustrate this thinking. Let's say a company has issued bonds, with a 10 percent interest rate. If inflation is low, say 2 percent, the bond investor makes roughly 8 percent on his money. But if inflation is 6 percent, then the investor is down to just 4 percent.

Nobody likes inflation, but bond investors dislike it even more. Why? Because it raises prices without any accompanying increase in growth and productivity.

Appendix II

Government Bailouts

As the last chapter indicated, politicians love to tinker with the free market. They act in such ways because they perceive that they will receive a benefit—getting re-elected—by catering to voting groups back home. And nowhere is this instinct more apparent than when a business is in danger of failing.

From the politicians' viewpoint, it makes sense to jump in with funding for the failing business. After all, investors could lose their assets and workers could lose their jobs. To lawmakers, this kind of pain must be avoided at all costs. And if the pain is widespread enough, lawmakers will join forces to pass legislation that usually throws money at the problem. This notion is often known by the phrase "too big to fail." And thus a bailout is born.

Most of the time, though, the real answer to a business in trouble is not federal tax funds, but a change in the law that led to the problem in the first place. That failure to change the law stems from—you guessed it—a lack of economic understanding on the part of lawmakers and the media.

A perfect case study of this was the $700 billion bailout of financial firms in 2008. With phrases such as "financial Armageddon" and "economic meltdown," financial firms, with the media's help, whipped up a crisis that pressured Congress into taking action.

Investment giants such as Bear, Stearns & Co. and Lehman Brothers saw their profits dropping like a stone. Because of their financial straits, banks stopped lending to them. (Big banks, such as Citicorp, weren't doing too well, either.) What brought them to such straits? That's where the tale of economic ignorance starts.

These firms' profits had disappeared because they weren't getting paid back for a certain type of loan. The chief trait of these so-called subprime loans was lax credit standards. Banks stopped requiring down payments and income minimums dropped. This led to an increase in defaults and foreclosures. It wasn't a problem, though, as long as home prices continued to rise as more people wanted houses. The banks could just put out another loan on the foreclosed property—at a higher price. Plus, subprime borrowers would reap a profit if they did sell their property.

If banks had taken on the risk of these subprime loans themselves, any default problems would have been limited to the lending world. But banks and investment houses saw a way to improve their profits by spreading the risk around. Banks would take these subprime loans, bundle them up and market them as securities backed by an asset, in these cases, a house.

Asset-backed securities had been around a long time, but they typically were made up of less risky investments assets, such as property where the borrower earned a substantial income and had made a large down payment. The subprime loans featured neither of these traits, but banks sold them off anyway, aided by credit analysts who gave these securities top-notch ratings.

Any problems, though, still would have been limited because once borrowers began defaulting, financial firms would have backed off and assumed less risk. But two government actions—one that was three-plus decades old and a more recent one—paved the way for the widespread looses and created a "financial Armageddon."

The first was the Community Reinvestment Act, passed in 1977. This law required lenders to make loans to "economically underserved" areas. In other words, banks shouldn't apply normal borrowing standards to these loans. Critics called the CRA "affirmative action for borrowers." Economic common sense would suggest that these lower credit standards led to a rise in defaults.

A 2000 Federal Reserve Board study of the default and non-performing rates confirms this common sense. Again, banks could absorb this unprofitability when home prices were rising. But when prices started to fall, the value of the asset they were carrying on their books fell, thus cutting into the bottom line.

President Clinton aggravated the problem when he made it policy to increase home ownership. The rate of ownership had hovered right around 65 percent for years, but this wasn't high enough for Clinton. He had a willing partner in his plan, moreover. He named Franklin Raines, his former budget director, to head up the Federal National Mortgage Association, or Fannie Mae. And his tenure from 1998 to 2003 saw the second government action occur, leading to the financial meltdown of 2008.

"It was under Raines' management that Fannie morphed from being a company in a sleepy business—issuing debt to buy mortgages from lenders—into a far more risky and exciting one," said The Motley Fool, an investment adviser.

Raines, with Clinton's plans and the Community Reinvestment Act, embarked on a subprime lending spree. Fannie Mae could get credit at lower rates because of its quasi-government status. So the higher rates charged subprime borrowers helped make Fannie Mae's bottom line look terrific.

But there were a couple of problems. One, returns from these loans were lower because of the higher default and foreclosure rates. And two, Raines ordered Fannie Mae execs to skirt normal accounting rules in order to pump up the profit levels. He took home $90 million in bonuses as a result of this scheme, but ended up paying back $24 million for "accounting errors."

Add to this the protection given Fannie Mae by powerful members of Congress—Rep. Barney Frank, D-MA, and Sen. Chris Dodd, D-CT—and all the pieces were in place to "bring the financial system to its knees," reported the Cincinnati Enquirer. Washington did begin to reign in Fannie Mae and its brother, Freddie Mac, with tighter standards and the firing of top execs. But Congress did nothing to change the Community Reinvestment Act, preferring instead to toss money at the problem.

So the credit problems of lenders will not disappear any time soon, because the government forces them to make loans that are prone to fail. And if those lenders are of any size at all, then the government will justify future bailouts with claims that the firm is "too big to fail." But economics suggests that a failure would be a better signal to lenders than any bailout of risky behavior.

INDEX